# FRANK QUITELY

## THE ART OF COMICS

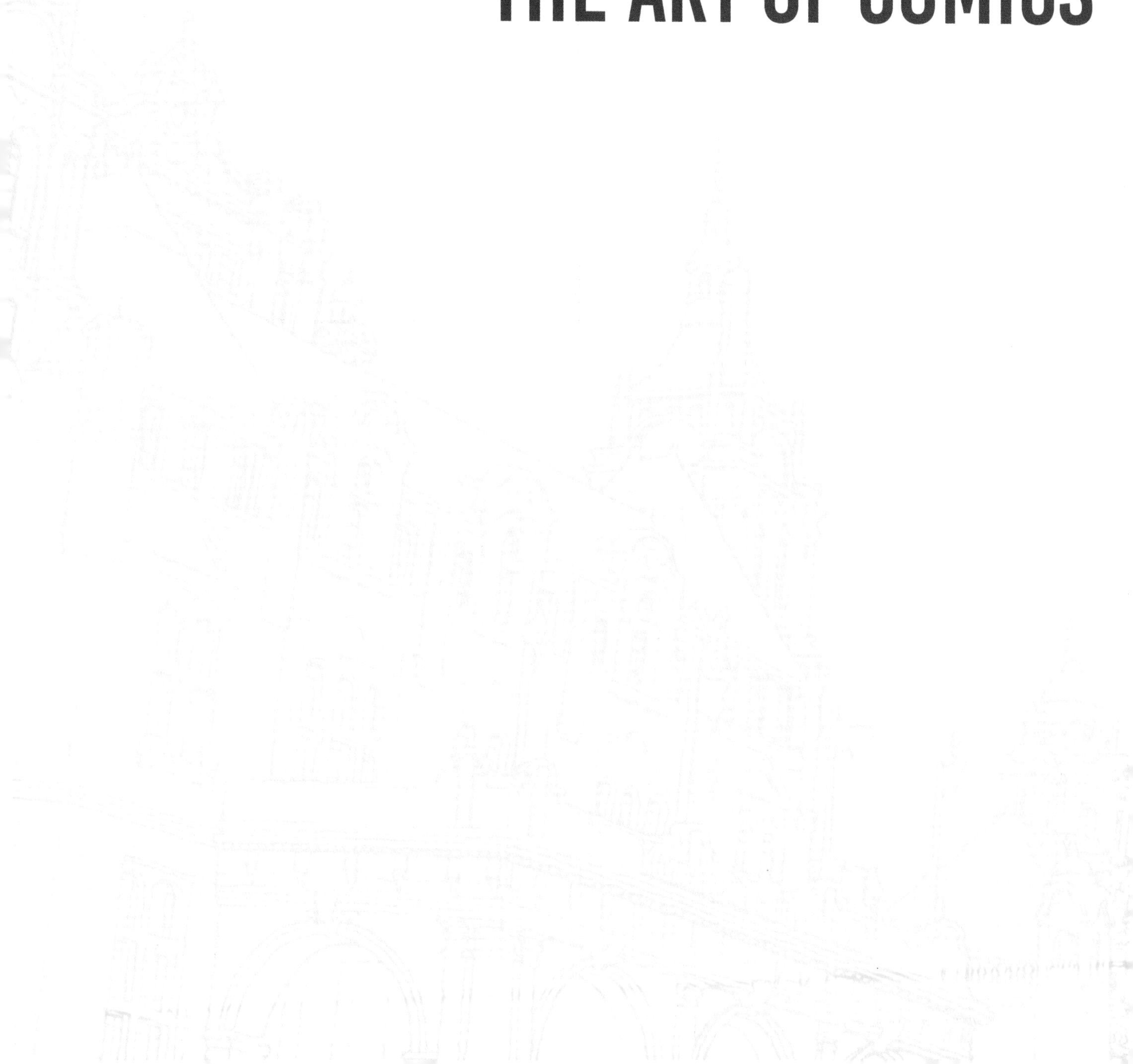

# FRANK QUITELY
## THE ART OF COMICS

Frank Quitely: The Art of Comics

Designed by Kirsty Hunter & Sha Nazir

First printing 2017

Published in Glasgow by (BHP Comics) Black Hearted Press Ltd.

Made in Scotland. Printed in Great Britain by Bell & Bain Ltd.

ISBN: 978-1-910775-08-0

A CIP catalogue reference for this book is available from the British Library.

**Ask your local comic or book shop to stock BHP Comics.**
**Visit BHPComics.com for more info.**

Opposite page: 'Wilhemina' (2011) illustration for Glasgow Comic Con.

# FRANK QUITELY
## THE ART OF COMICS

## FOREWORD

Comics were invented in Glasgow. It is fitting then that Glasgow—the South Side to be precise—should be home to Frank Quitely, known worldwide for drawing *Batman*, *Superman*, *Judge Dredd* and *X-Men*.

To take the story back to its opening frame, it can be argued that humans have always told tales with pictures, from hieroglyphs to Roman road-slabs to medieval manuscripts, although less well known is the fact that here too Glasgow is a world-beater. The planet's best miscellany of early picture books, the Stirling Maxwell collection, is housed in Glasgow University Library, with over 2000 volumes putting text together with images to tell us about life, draw conclusions, and narrate the bigger picture. One such example is George Wither's 1635 *A Collection of Emblemes* in which a skeleton protagonist reminds us of the greatest narrative of all, the one that takes us from life to death.

Why then is *The Glasgow Looking Glass* the world's first comic, and why Glasgow? It was in 1825 that William Heath, the London-born caricaturist, seized the opportunity offered by the new technology of lithography to create an illustrated journal that mocked society, titillated with picture-puns and told stories that were 'to be continued'. If a modern comic has to be mass produced so we can fold it up and take it home (or not fold it for many fans), then this was the world's first, predating other contenders, including *Obadiah Oldbuck*, America's first, from as late as 1842.

As an industrial city Glasgow had the technology, but also the ready-for-a-laugh punters of the drinking classes. The city also produced *The Glasgow Punch* in 1832, nine years before the London one, and in 1906 the *Looking Glass* was briefly reissued and referred to as *The Scotch Punch*. Cartooning caricature continued to flourish, up to and beyond Bud Neill's Lobey Dosser and his tales of the Wild West, including the Clydebank cannibals. And just up the road in Dundee, DC Thomson were enthralling old and young alike, including a certain Vincent Deighan, with the *Beano*, *Dandy*, *Broons* and *Oor Wullie*.

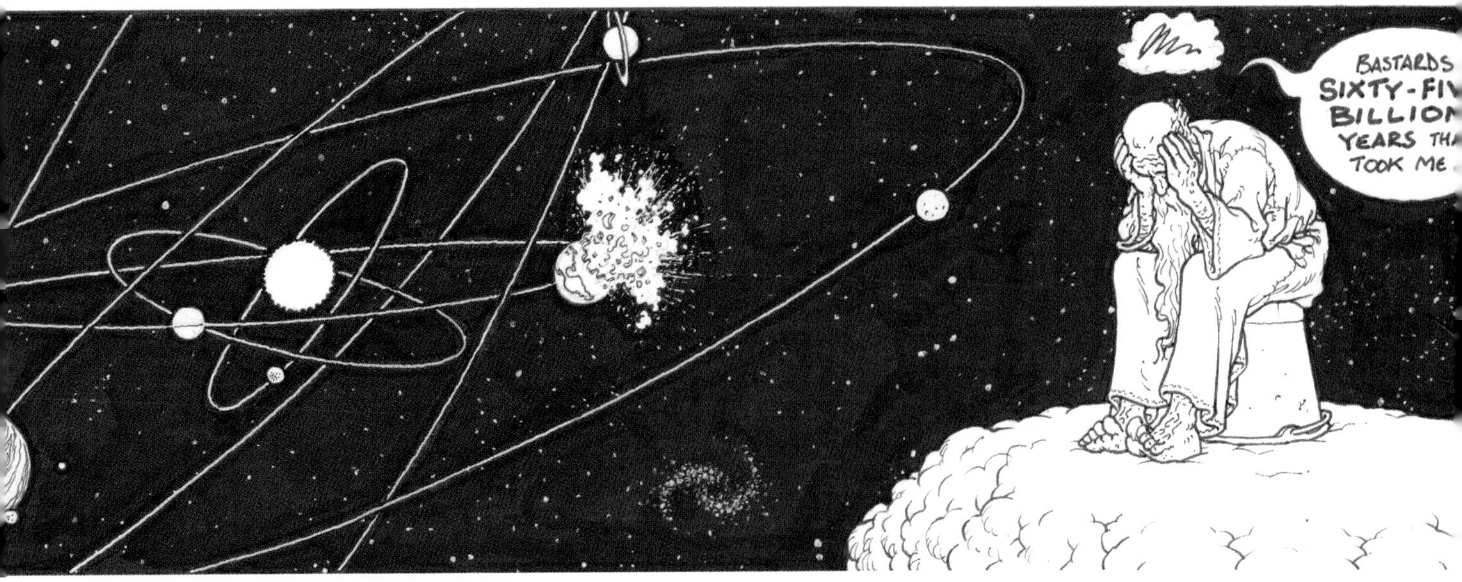
BASTARDS
SIXTY-FI
BILLION
YEARS TH
TOOK ME

On the serious side (but not always), Glasgow was to become the contemporary art Turner Prize mecca, and would be home to Martin Boyce, David Shrigley, Christine Borland and Douglas Gordon, all of whom, like Frank Quitely (albeit briefly) studied at the Glasgow School of Art. The city's art museums, part of the best civic collection in Europe, were making the work of Dali and Rembrandt, alongisde more contemporary practitioners like David Hockney and Alasdair Gray, available to all.

Such is the backcloth to the artistic beginnings of Vincent Deighan, born in 1968 and educated at St. Brides High School in East Kilbride. It was in the early 1990s that he spoofed ***The Broons*** as ***The Greens*** for the underground comic ***Electric Soup***, and realising that, quite frankly, his work might offend his family, he hid behind the spoonerism penname. In 1996 Frank Quitely started working for DC, initially on ***Flex Mentallo***, before going on to ***The Sandman***, ***Pax Americana***, and ***We3***.

Frank Quitely's output is vast and varied, but for many it is the ***Superman*** and Batman duo that makes him the boy wonder of comics. In both cases Frank Quitely and his collaborators continue a comics canon that dates back to the 1930s, but in both cases they undermine the canon with their own iconoclastic touches, be it taking Batman away from Gotham and into Scotland (***Batman: The Scottish Connection*** first appeared in 1998), or the anti-establishment nuances of the ***All-Star Superman*** (2005 onwards), indicated from the outset by the cheeky acrostic formed by the title's initials.

The wit of the writing is matched by that of the drawing style. Frank Quitely largely works with time-consuming traditional methods, aided when needed by high-tech implements. His page-layout and panel-plays create the movement that guides the viewer, while his close-up attention to detail is meticulous and busy: look out for the background details, be it the large lady emptying the buffet, the falling plant pot knocked over by the leaping assailant, or the crossed-legged ***femme fatale*** seated on Grant Morrison's thumb.

Grant Morrison appears within this catalogue not only as the subject of Quitely's artwork, but more importantly as one of his most frequent collaborators. Frank Quitely has worked with many of the icons of comics, including Alan Grant, Bruce Jones and Neil Gaiman, but it is his partnerships with Morrison and with Mark Miller – here for example on ***Jupiter's Legacy*** – that are best known. It is a holy trinity that brings us back to Glasgow, mirroring the ***Looking Glass*** and placing Scotland at the heart of comics.

In return Glasgow that has brought recognition to its native phenomenon, drawing attention to the city's creations and creators, but also to comics as a form. Prior to the current Kelvingrove and Clydebank displays, in 2016 The Hunterian's ***Comic Invention*** put Lichtenstein next to Rembrandt next to Frank Quitely, demonstrating that his stand-alone artwork is worthy of any gallery. In 2017 Frank Quitely will be awarded an honorary PhD from the University of Glasgow, making him the first comics artist to receive such an accolade from an Ancient University, and meaning that the cape for Glasgow's comics superhero, Dr Quitely, alter-ego of the mild-mannered Mr Deighan, will be an academic gown.

**Laurence Grove**
*Professor of French and Text / Image Studies*
*Director, Stirling Maxwell Centre*
*University of Glasgow.*

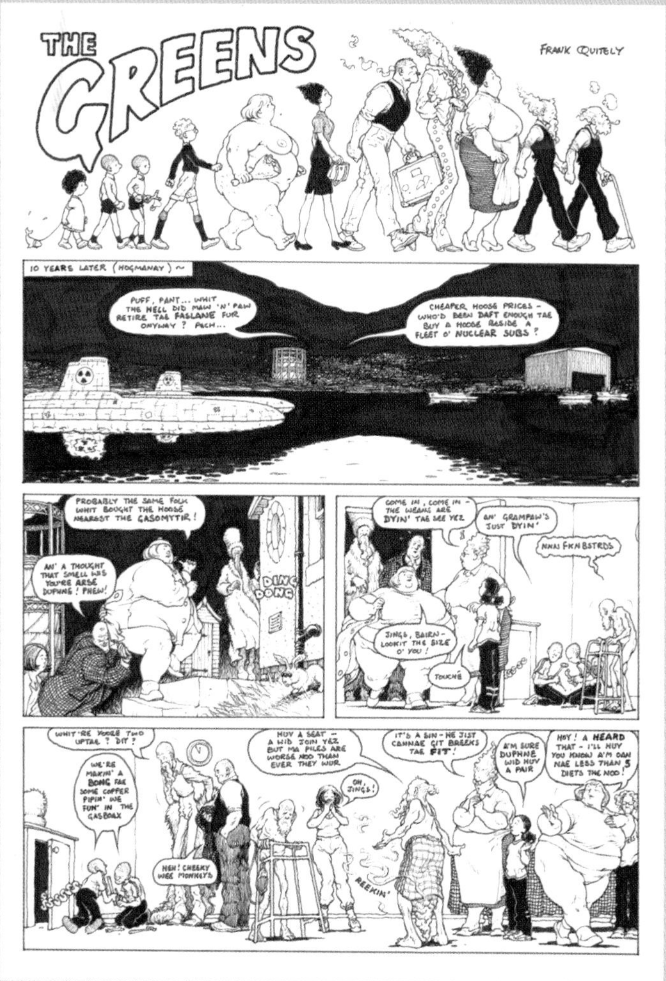
THE GREENS
FRANK QUITELY
10 YEARS LATER (HOGMANAY) ~
PUFF, PANT... WHIT THE HELL DID MAW 'N' PAW RETIRE TAE FASLANE FUR ONYWAY? PECH...
CHEAPER HOOSE PRICES - WHO'D BEEN DAFT ENOUGH TAE BUY A HOOSE BESIDE A FLEET O' NUCLEAR SUBS?
PROBABLY THE SAME FOLK WHIT BOUGHT THE HOOSE NEAREST THE GASOMYTIR!
AN' A THOUGHT THAT SMELL WIS YOU'RE ARSE DUPHNE! PHEW!
DING DONG
COME IN, COME IN - THE WEANS ARE DYIN' TAE SEE YEZ
AN' GRAMPAW'S JUST DYIN'
NNN FKN BSTRDS
JINGS, BAIRN - LOOKIT THE SIZE O' YOU!
TOUCHÉ
WHIT'RE YOORE TWO UPTAE? DIT?
WE'RE MAKIN' A BONG FAE SOME COPPER PIPIN' WE FUN' IN THE GASBOAX
HEH! CHEEKY WEE MONKEYS
HUV A SEAT - A WID JOIN YEZ BUT MA PILES ARE WORSE NOO THAN EVER THEY WUR
OH, JINGS!
REEKIN'
IT'S A SIN - HE JIST CANNAE GIT BREEKS TAE FIT!
A'M SURE DUPHNE WID HUV A PAIR
HOY! A HEARD THAT - I'LL HUV YOU KNOW A'M OAN NAE LESS THAN 5 DIETS THE NOO!

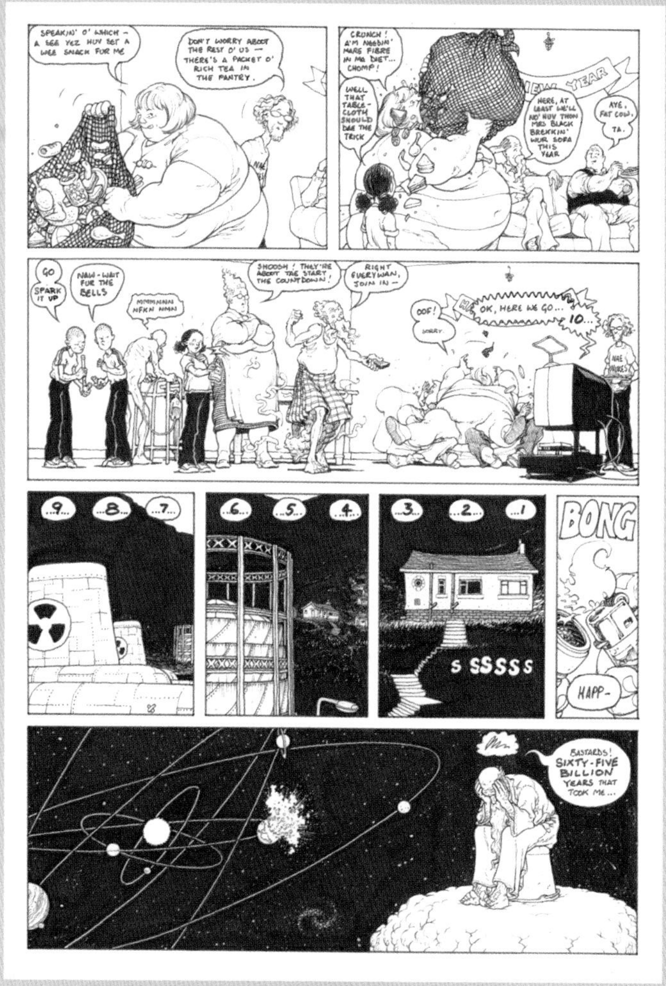
SPEAKIN' O' WHICH - A SEE YEZ HUV SET A WEE SNACK FUR ME
DON'T WORRY ABOOT THE REST O' US — THERE'S A PACKET O' RICH TEA IN THE PANTRY.
CRUNCH! A'M NEEDIN' MAIR FIBRE IN MA DIET... CHOMP!
WELL THAT TABLE-CLOTH SHOULD DAE THE TRICK
NEW YEAR
HERE, AT LEAST WE'LL NO' HUV THON MRS BLACK BREKKIN' WUR SOFA THIS YEAR
AYE, FAT COW.
TA.
GO SPARK IT UP
NAW - WAIT FUR THE BELLS
MMMNNN NFKN NMN
SHOOSH! THEY'RE ABOOT TAE START THE COUNTDOWN!
RIGHT EVERYWAN, JOIN IN —
OOF!
SORRY.
OK, HERE WE GO... 10...
NAE NUKES
...9... ...8... ...7...
...6... ...5... ...4...
...3... ...2... ...1
S SSSSS
BONG
HAPP-
BASTARDS! SIXTY-FIVE BILLION YEARS THAT TOOK ME...

Above and opposite page: ***Electric Soup***, 'The Greens' #1 (anthology, 1990).
Pen and Black Ink

Quitely's first published strip, 'The Greens', affectionately parodies classic comic, ***The Broons*** (DC Thomson). The final panel replaces the traditional Wullie sitting on his bucket, with a sulking God.

THE GREENS

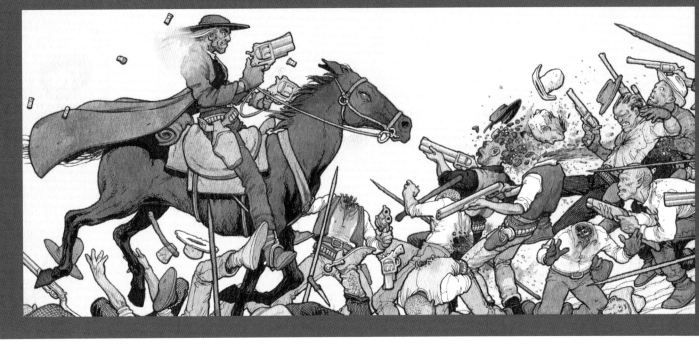

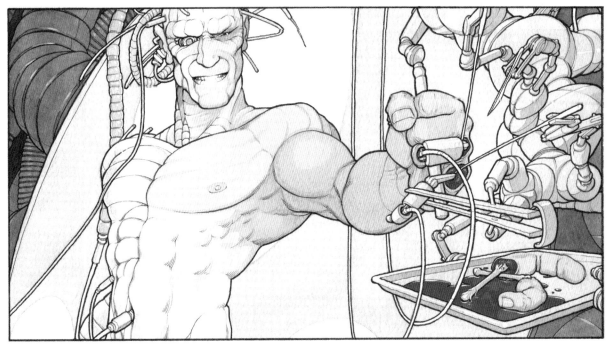

Top: Selected panel from *Judge Dredd Megazine*, vol.2, 'Bad Moon Rising' #29 (writer: Gordon Rennie, Rebellion, 1993) p24. Ink, watercolour and gouache.

Above: Selected panel from *Judge Dredd Megazine*, vol.2, "Shimura" #37 (writer: Robbie Morrison, Rebellion, 1993) p.23. Ink, watercolour and gouache.

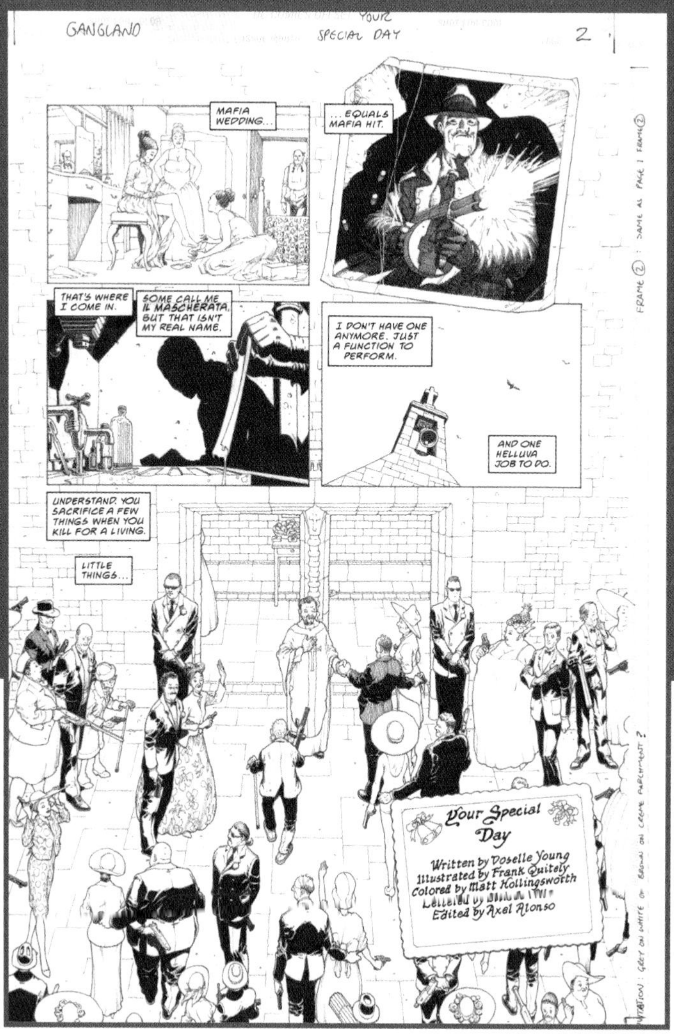
GANGLAND
YOUR SPECIAL DAY
2
MAFIA WEDDING...
...EQUALS MAFIA HIT.
THAT'S WHERE I COME IN.
SOME CALL ME IL MASCHERATA. BUT THAT ISN'T MY REAL NAME.
I DON'T HAVE ONE ANYMORE. JUST A FUNCTION TO PERFORM.
AND ONE HELLUVA JOB TO DO.
UNDERSTAND. YOU SACRIFICE A FEW THINGS WHEN YOU KILL FOR A LIVING.
LITTLE THINGS...
Your Special Day
Written by Doselle Young
Illustrated by Frank Quitely
Colored by Matt Hollingsworth
Edited by Axel Alonso

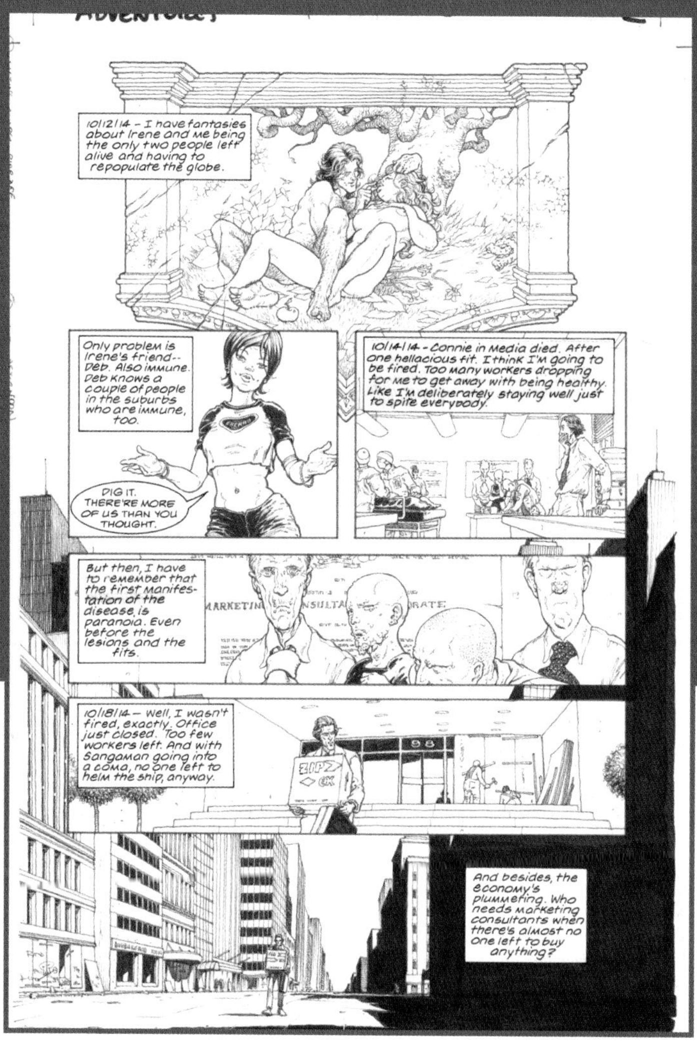
10/12/14 – I have fantasies about Irene and me being the only two people left alive and having to repopulate the globe.
Only problem is Irene's friend-- Deb. Also immune. Deb knows a couple of people in the suburbs who are immune, too.
DIG IT. THERE'RE MORE OF US THAN YOU THOUGHT.
10/14/14 - Connie in Media died. After one hellacious fit. I think I'm going to be fired. Too many workers dropping for me to get away with being healthy. Like I'm deliberately staying well just to spite everybody.
But then, I have to remember that the first manifestation of the disease is paranoia. Even before the lesions and the fits.
10/18/14 – Well, I wasn't fired, exactly. Office just closed. Too few workers left. And with Sangaman going into a coma, no one left to helm the ship, anyway.
And besides, the economy's plummeting. Who needs marketing consultants when there's almost no one left to buy anything?

Left: ***Gangland***, #1 'Your Special Day' (writer: Doselle Young, anthology, Vertigo, 1997) p.2. Pen and black ink.

Below: ***Strange Adventures***, vol.2 #1 'Immune' (writer: Robert Rodi, anthology, Vertigo, 1999) p.2. Pen and black ink.

Both of these pages feature instances where Quitely mimics other mediums in his comic art: panel two of 'Your Special Day' takes the form of a weathered photo while in 'Immune', a character's edenic fantasies are shown as a frieze.

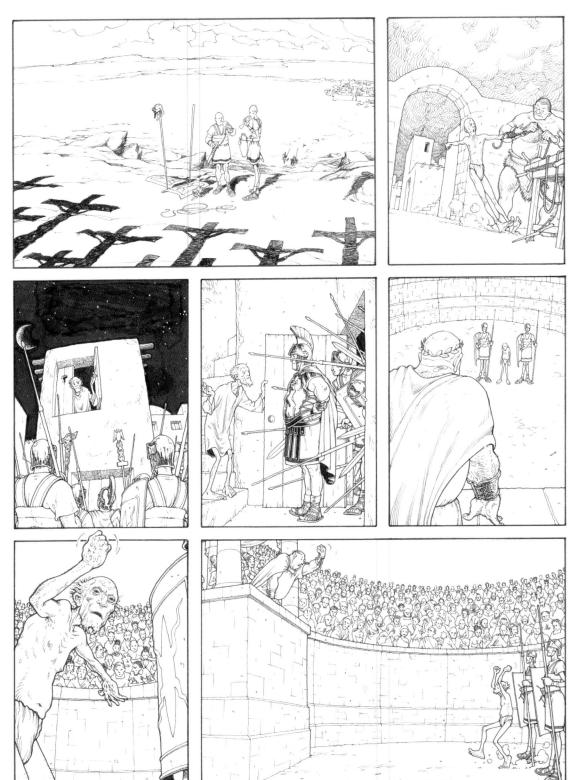

61%

WEIRDOS
DALI
2
139
BURNING GIRAFFES.
IN PARIS, HE ALSO PUT THE FINAL TOUCHES ON HIS FINEST CREATION: HIMSELF.
AH, MY MUS-TACHE...
...IT IS LIKE THE ANTENNAE OF INSECTS, IT PULLS IDEAS OUT OF THE AIR...
139
61%

Freaks
Elephant Man
39
THE ELEPHANT MAN
UNFORTUNATELY, THIS MEMORY WAS PROBABLY FALSE. GENTLE JOHN MERRICK'S FIRST REAL MEMORY WAS VERY LIKELY OF SUFFERING IN A LONDON WORKHOUSE FOR THE POOR.
--UNDER THE CARE OF A VARIETY OF IMPOVERISHED SHOWMEN WHO PUT HIM ON DISPLAY TO EARN DRINKING MONEY.
HIS RIGHT ARM WAS A BIG USELESS CLUB. HIS BODY WAS COVERED WITH LARGE CABBAGE-LIKE TUMORS. AWFUL GROWTHS ON HIS HUGE, MISSHAPEN HEAD AL-MOST COMPLETELY COVERED ONE EYE AND PERMANENTLY FIXED HIS MOUTH INTO A DROOLING HOLE SO HE COULD NEITHER FROWN NOR SMILE.
HIS CRIPPLED HIPS MADE IT IMPOSSIBLE FOR MERRICK TO ESCAPE HIS TORMEN-TORS, AND HIS TUMOROUS SKIN STANK IF NOT WASHED DAILY -WHICH, OF COURSE, IT NEVER WAS.
39

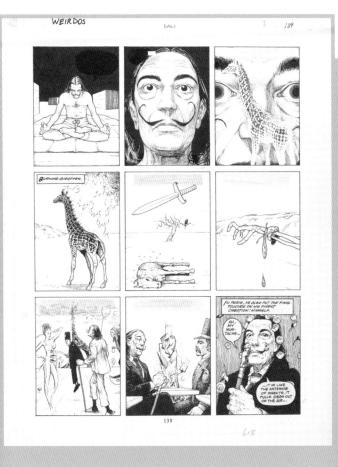

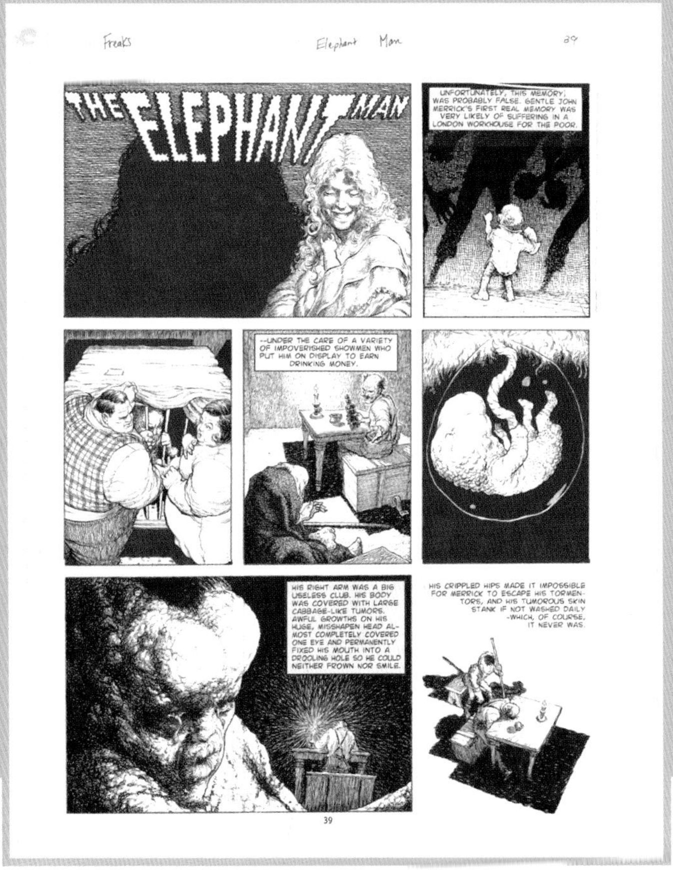

Left (top): ***The Big Book of Weirdos***, 'Dali' (writer: Carl Posey, Vertigo, 1995) p.2. Pen and black ink.

Left (bottom): ***The Big Book of Freaks***, 'The Elephant Man' (writer: Gahan Wilson, Vertigo, 1996) p.39. Pen and black ink.

Far left: ***The Big Book of Martyrs***, 'St. Polycarp: The Cult of Saints' (writer: John Wagner, Vertigo, 1997) p48. Pen and black ink.

In the central panel of the page , Quitely plays up the ridiculous juxtiposition of the fragile old man with the excessively-armed Roman phalanx, making his plight both comedic and tragic.

# FLEX MENTALLO

FLEX 4 6
GRANT MORRISON, WRITER
FRANK QUITELY, ARTIST
TOM McCRAW, COLORIST
ELLIE deVILLE, LETTERER
AXEL ALONSO EDITOR
AFTER THE 'FACT'
PART FOUR
We aRe all UFOs
6

FLEX 1 4
BOSS? YOU OKAY? YOU LOOK KINDA PALE.
WHAT'S UP, BOSS?
THE FACT IS:
THE "FACT"? HERE?
IMPOSSIBLE!
THINK AGAIN, WAXWORKER!
THE FACT IS: NOTHING IS IMPOSSIBLE!
HAVEN'T SEEN THIS STUFF FOR AGES. THESE ARE ACTUALLY BRILLIANT.
LOOK!
WHEN YOU'RE A KID YOU JUST DO IT. YOU DON'T EVEN THINK ABOUT IT. IT'S PURE. IT'S TOTALLY PURE.
SHIT! I'VE GOT TO STOP LOOKING AT ALL THIS.
BE HERE ALL NIGHT.


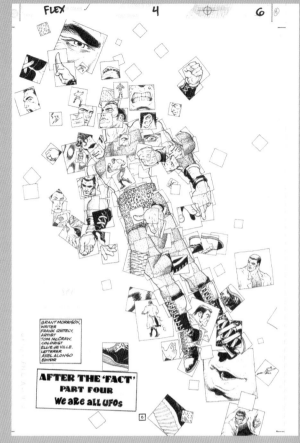

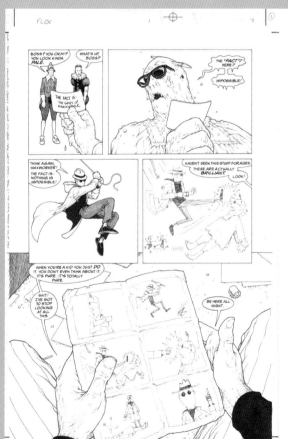

Left: ***Flex Mentallo*** #4 (writer: Grant Morrison, Vertigo, 1996) p.6. Pen and black ink.

Below: ***Flex Mentallo*** #1 (writer: Grant Morrison, Vertigo, 1996) p.9. Pen and black ink.

Right: ***Flex Mentallo*** #2 (writer: Grant Morrison, Vertigo, 1996) p.5. Pen and black ink.

SHOT FOR COLOR ✓ SHOT FOR CODE
TITLE: FLEX ISSUE/MONTH: 2 PAGE 5

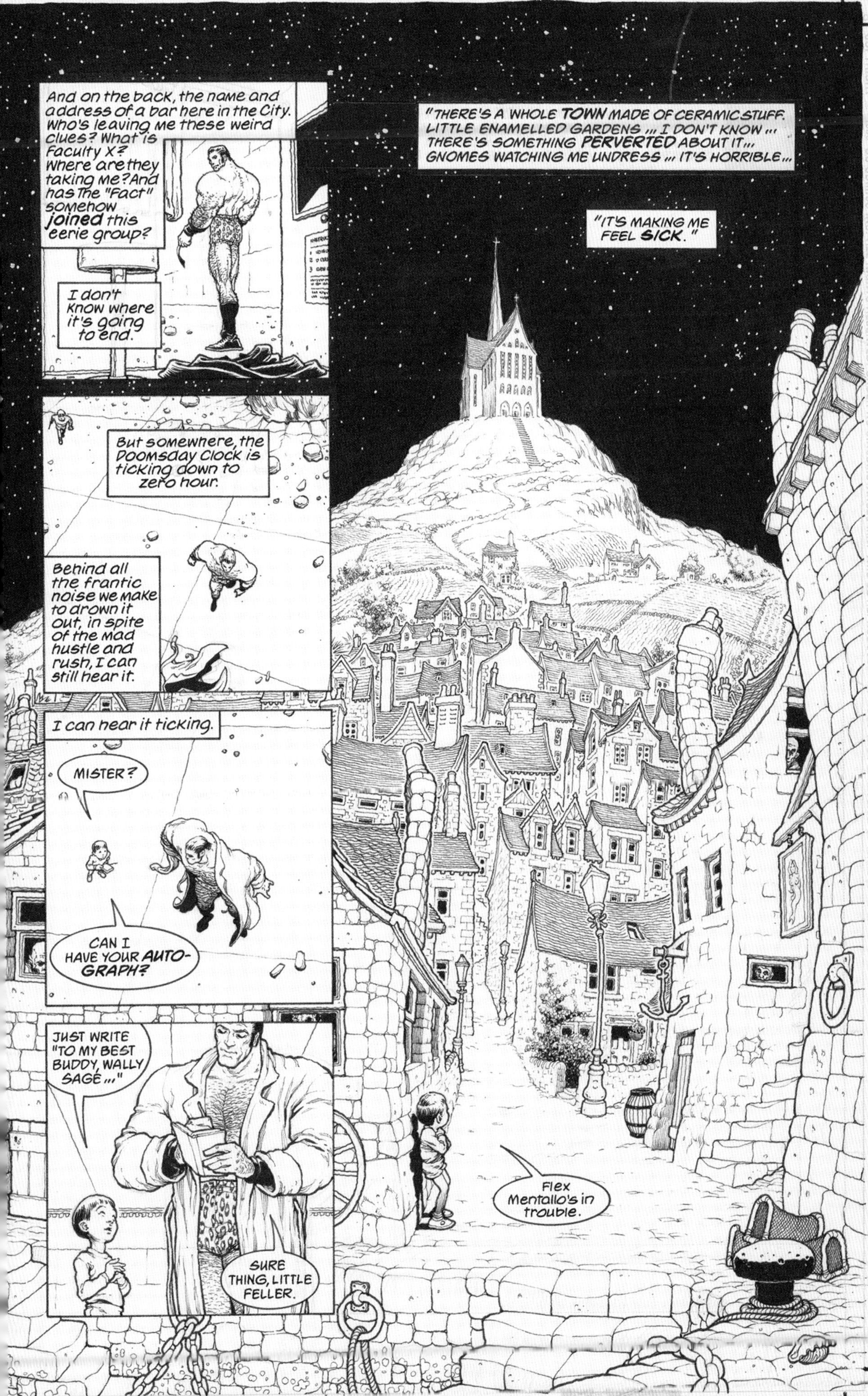

And on the back, the name and address of a bar here in the City. Who's leaving me these weird clues? What is Faculty X? Where are they taking me? And has the "Fact" somehow joined this eerie group?
I don't know where it's going to end.
But somewhere, the Doomsday Clock is ticking down to zero hour.
Behind all the frantic noise we make to drown it out, in spite of the mad hustle and rush, I can still hear it.
I can hear it ticking.
MISTER?
CAN I HAVE YOUR AUTO-GRAPH?
JUST WRITE "TO MY BEST BUDDY, WALLY SAGE..."
SURE THING, LITTLE FELLER.
"THERE'S A WHOLE TOWN MADE OF CERAMIC STUFF. LITTLE ENAMELLED GARDENS... I DON'T KNOW... THERE'S SOMETHING PERVERTED ABOUT IT... GNOMES WATCHING ME UNDRESS... IT'S HORRIBLE...
"IT'S MAKING ME FEEL SICK."
Flex Mentallo's in trouble.

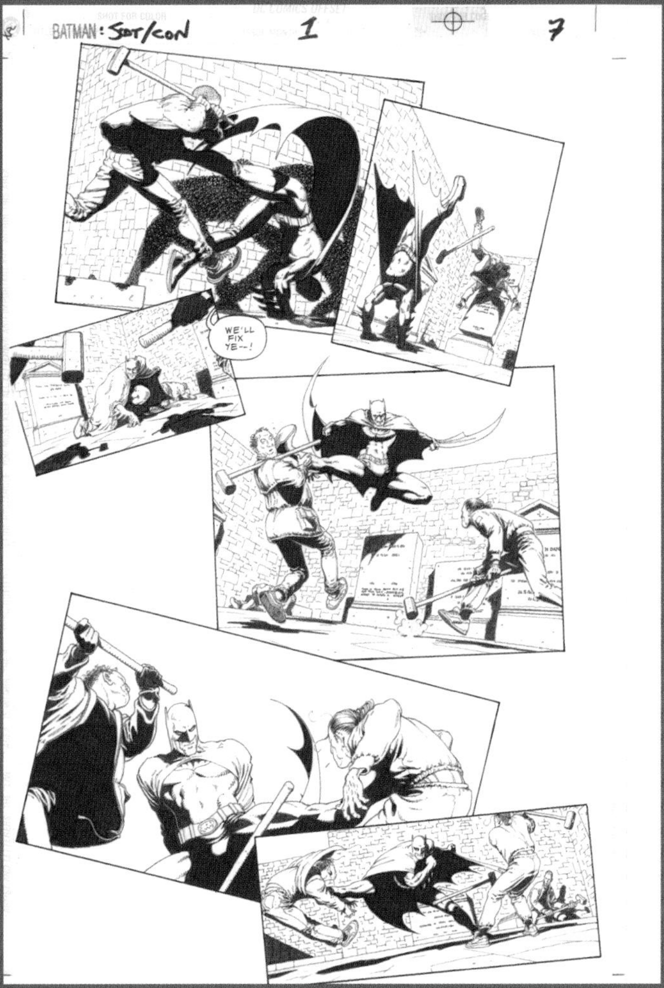
BATMAN: SOT/CON 1 7
WE'LL FIX YE—!

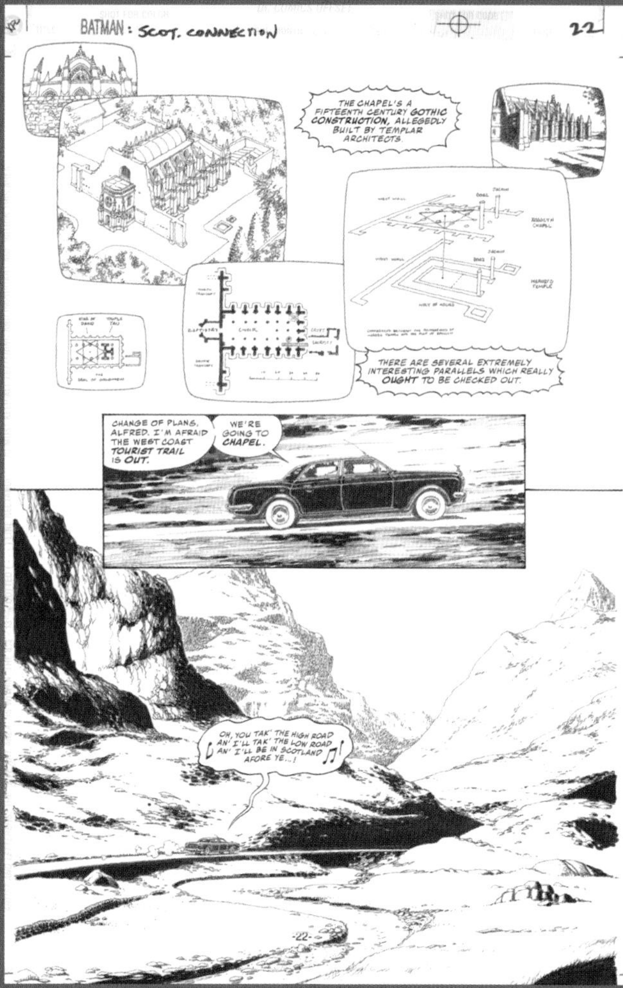
BATMAN: SCOT. CONNECTION 22
THE CHAPEL'S A FIFTEENTH CENTURY GOTHIC CONSTRUCTION, ALLEGEDLY BUILT BY TEMPLAR ARCHITECTS.
THERE ARE SEVERAL EXTREMELY INTERESTING PARALLELS WHICH REALLY OUGHT TO BE CHECKED OUT.
CHANGE OF PLANS, ALFRED. I'M AFRAID THE WEST COAST TOURIST TRAIL IS OUT.
WE'RE GOING TO CHAPEL.
OH, YOU TAK' THE HIGH ROAD AN' I'LL TAK' THE LOW ROAD AN' I'LL BE IN SCOTLAND AFORE YE...!
-22-

Above (Left to Right):

***Batman: The Scottish Connection*** (writer: Alan Grant, DC Comics, 1998) p.7. Pen and black ink.

***Batman: The Scottish Connection*** (writer: Alan Grant, DC Comics, 1998) p.7. Pen and black ink.

Grant and Quitely rarely depict Batman in his cowl and cape, instead focusing on the dark knight's investigative skills.

***Batman and Robin*** #1 (writer: Grant Morrison, DC Comics, 2009) p.18. Digital inks.

***Batman and Robin*** #1 (writer: Grant Morrison, DC Comics, 2009) p.22. Digital inks.

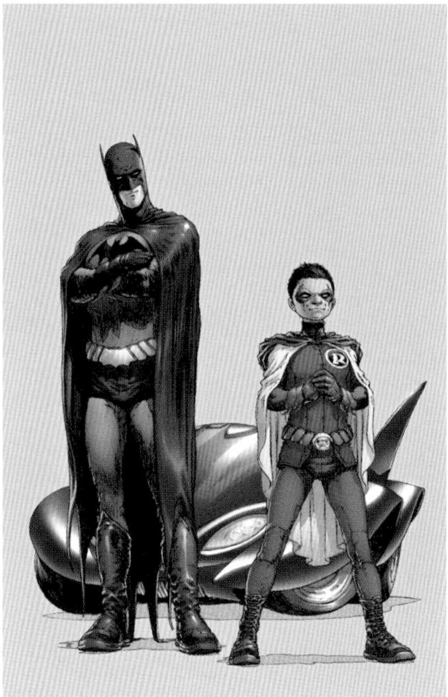

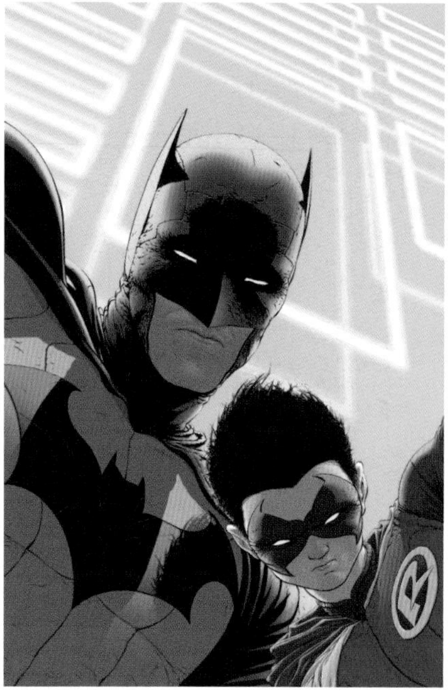

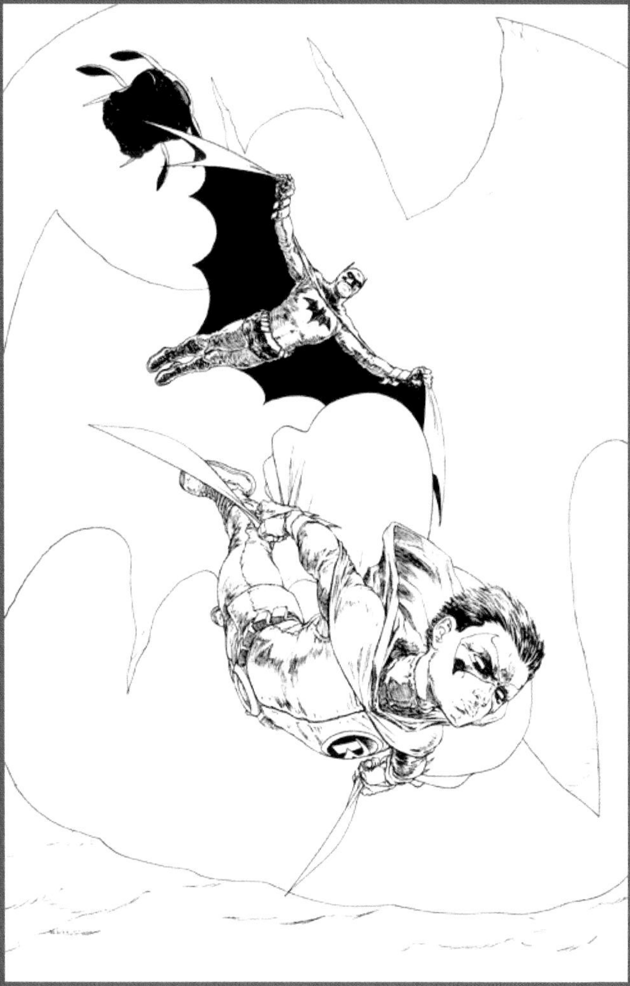

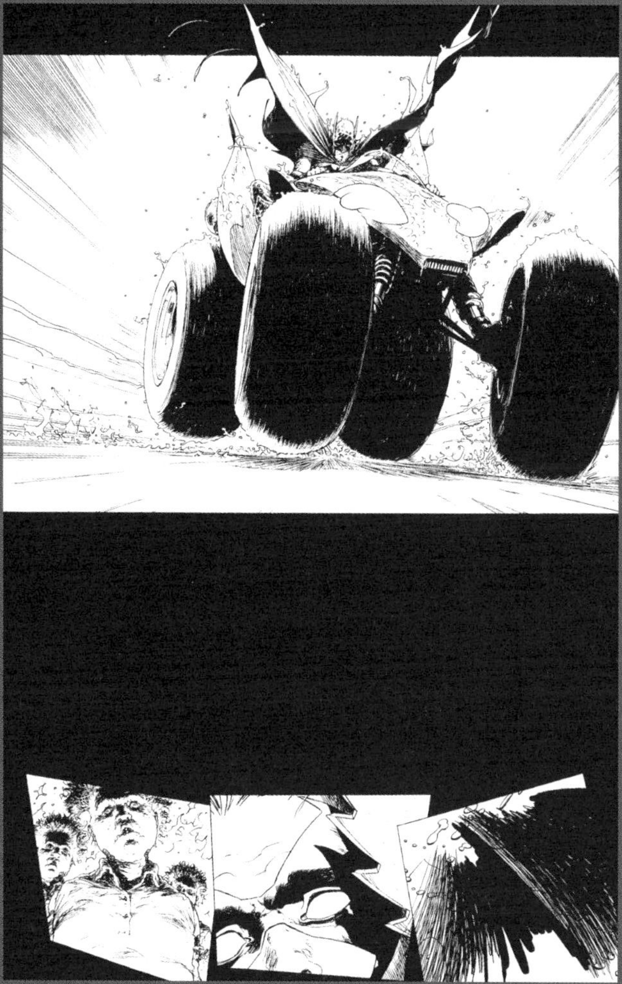

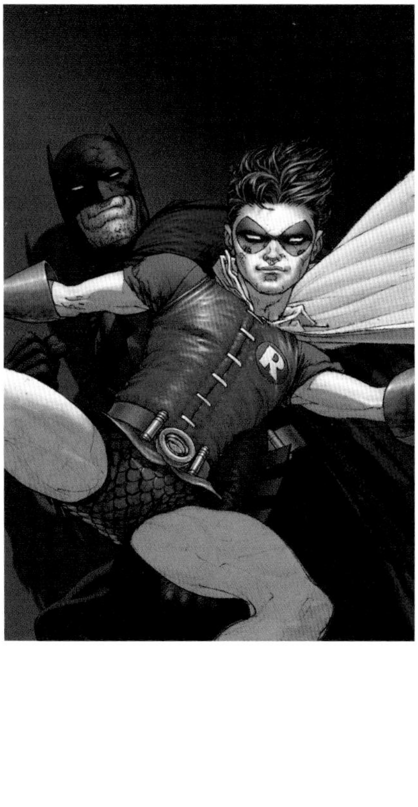

Below (Left to Right)

***Batman and Robin*** vol.1, 'Batman Reborn' #1-3 (writer: Grant Morrison, DC Comics, 2009) cover.

***Batman Incorporated***, #1 (writer: Grant Morrison, DC Comics, 2012) variant cover. Finished art, full colour digital.

***All Star Batman and Robin the Boy Wonder*** (writer: Frank Miller, DC Comics, 2008) variant cover. Finished art, full colour digital

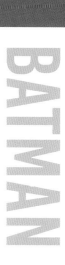

# BATMAN

NEW X MEN 122 12

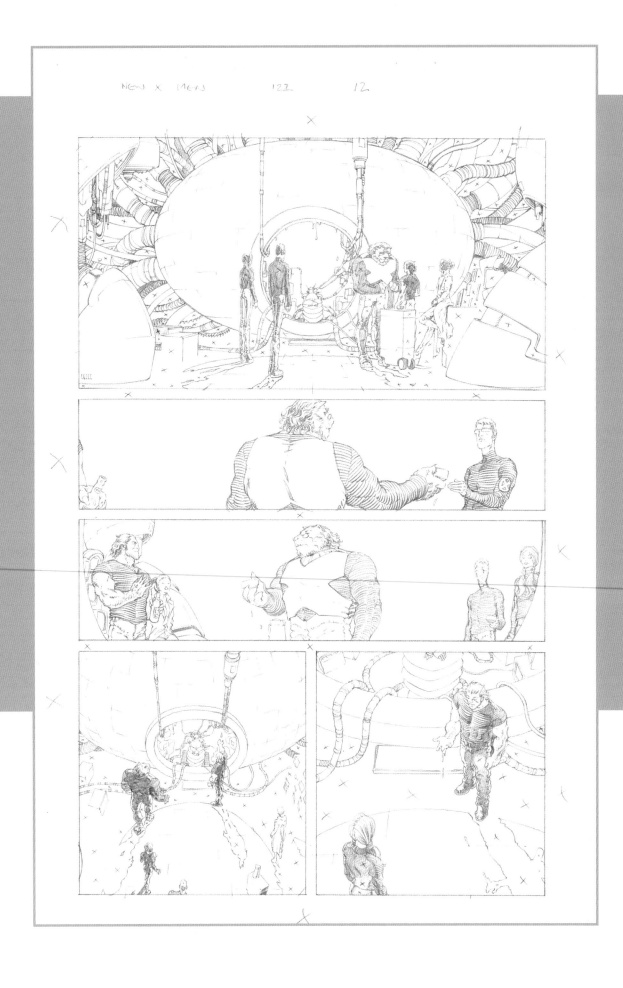

E IS FOR EXTINCTION
ONE OF THREE
DIRECT EDITION
MARVEL
NEW X-MEN
JUL 2001 114 GRANT MORRISON ■ FRANK QUITELY ■ TIM TOWNSEND
WWW.MARVEL.COM

COVERS - ILLUSTRATION QUALITY
PRINTS AT 69%
FRANK QUITELY
TITLE
#
MONTH
MARVEL COMICS

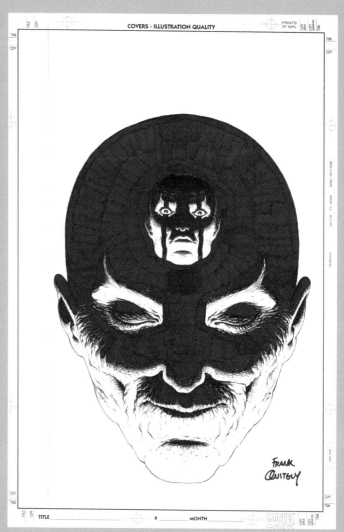

Above: ***New X-Men*** vol.1, #114 (writer: Grant Morrison, Marvel, 2002) cover. Full colour digital.

Right: ***New X-Men*** vol.1, #121 (writer: Grant Morrison, Marvel, 2002) cover. Pen and black ink.

Opposite page. ***New X-Men*** vol.1, #122, (writer: Grant Morrison, Marvel, 2002) p.12. Pen and black ink.

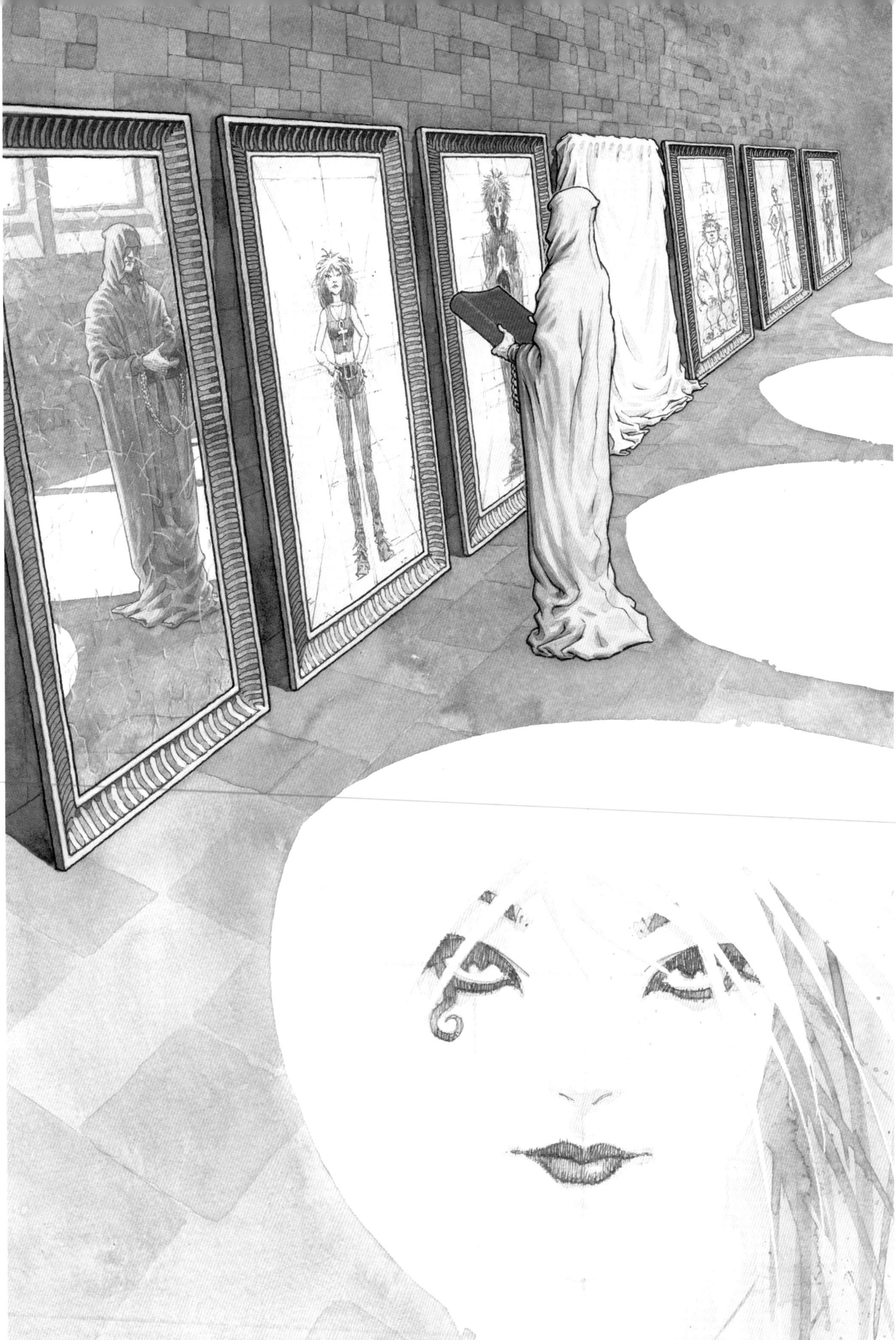

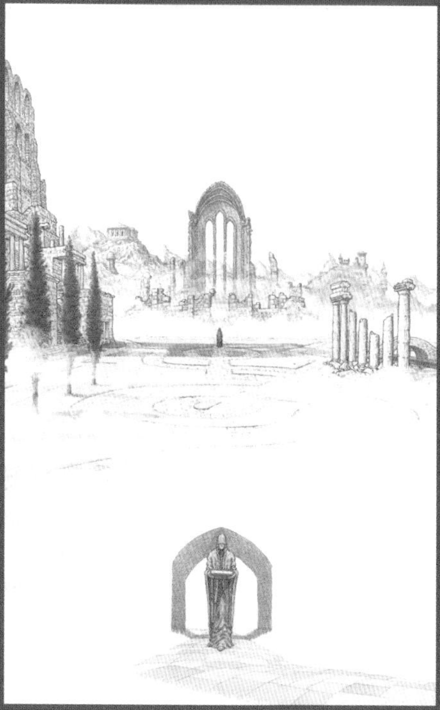

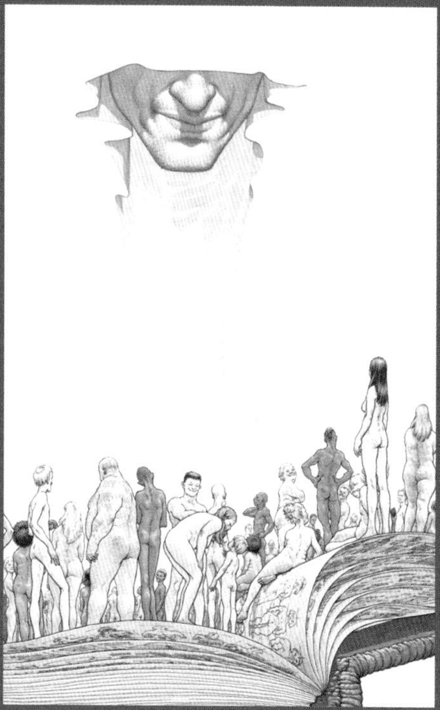

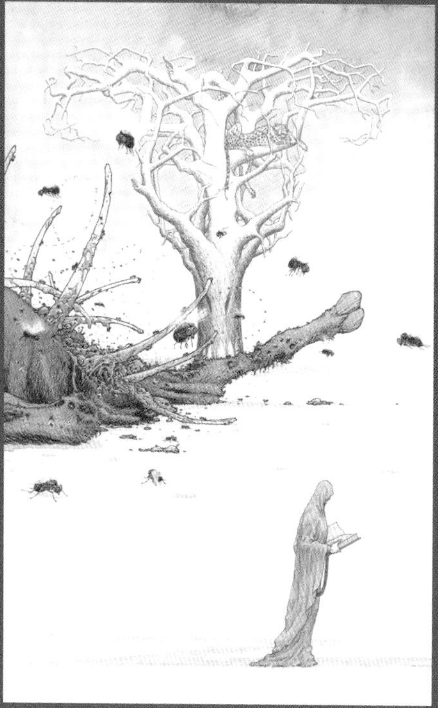

This page:

Above: ***The Sandman: Endless Nights,*** 'Chapter VII: Destiny' (writer: Neil Gaiman and various artists, Vertigo / DC Comics, 2003) pp.1, 6, 7. Ink, watercolour and gouache.

Right: ***The Sandman: Endless Nights,*** 'Chapter VII: Destiny' (writer: Neil Gaiman and various artists, Vertigo / DC Comics, 2003) retail poster, watercolour and gouache.

Opposite page: ***The Sandman: Endless Nights,*** 'Chapter VII: Destiny' (writer: Neil Gaiman and various artists, Vertigo / DC Comics, 2003) p.3. Ink, watercolour and gouache.

# SANDMAN

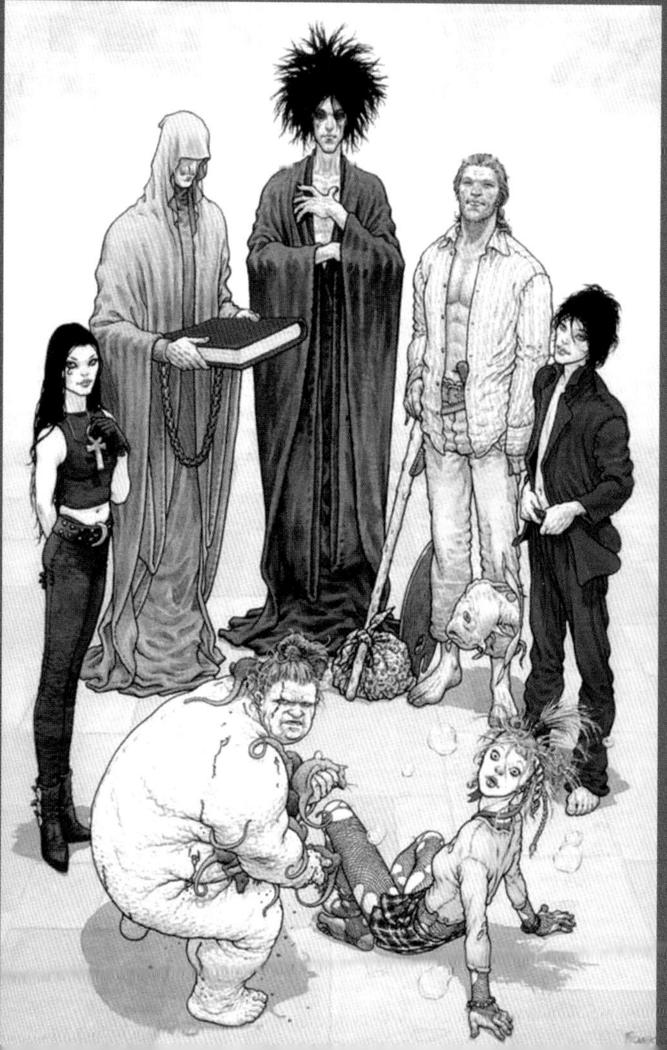

WE3 10

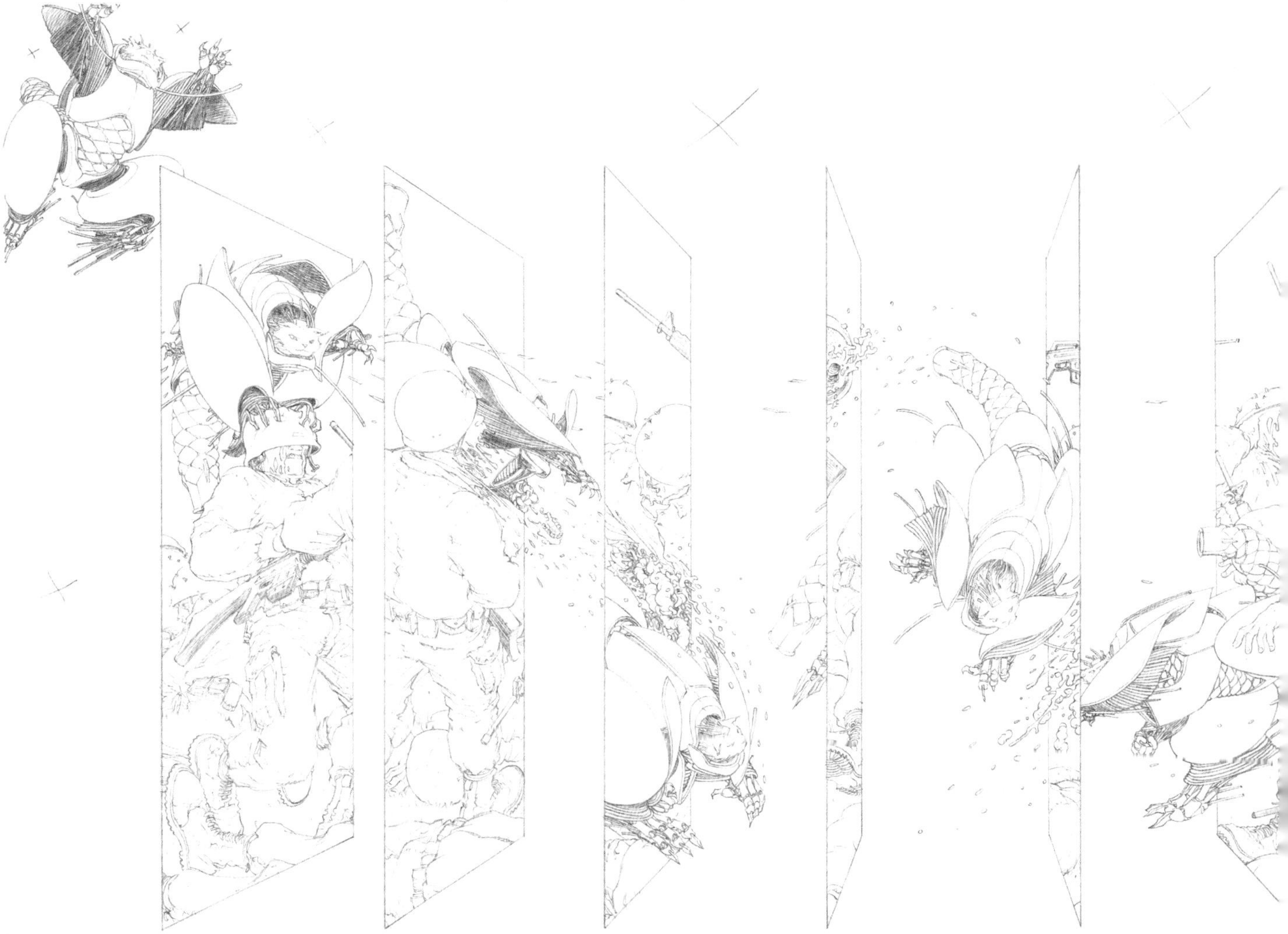

Left: *We3: The Deluxe Edition* (writer:
Grant Morrison, Vertigo, 2004–2005)
pp.54-55. Pencil.

Right: *We3: The Deluxe Edition*
 (writer: Grant Morrison, Vertigo,
2011) cover. Digital.

WE3

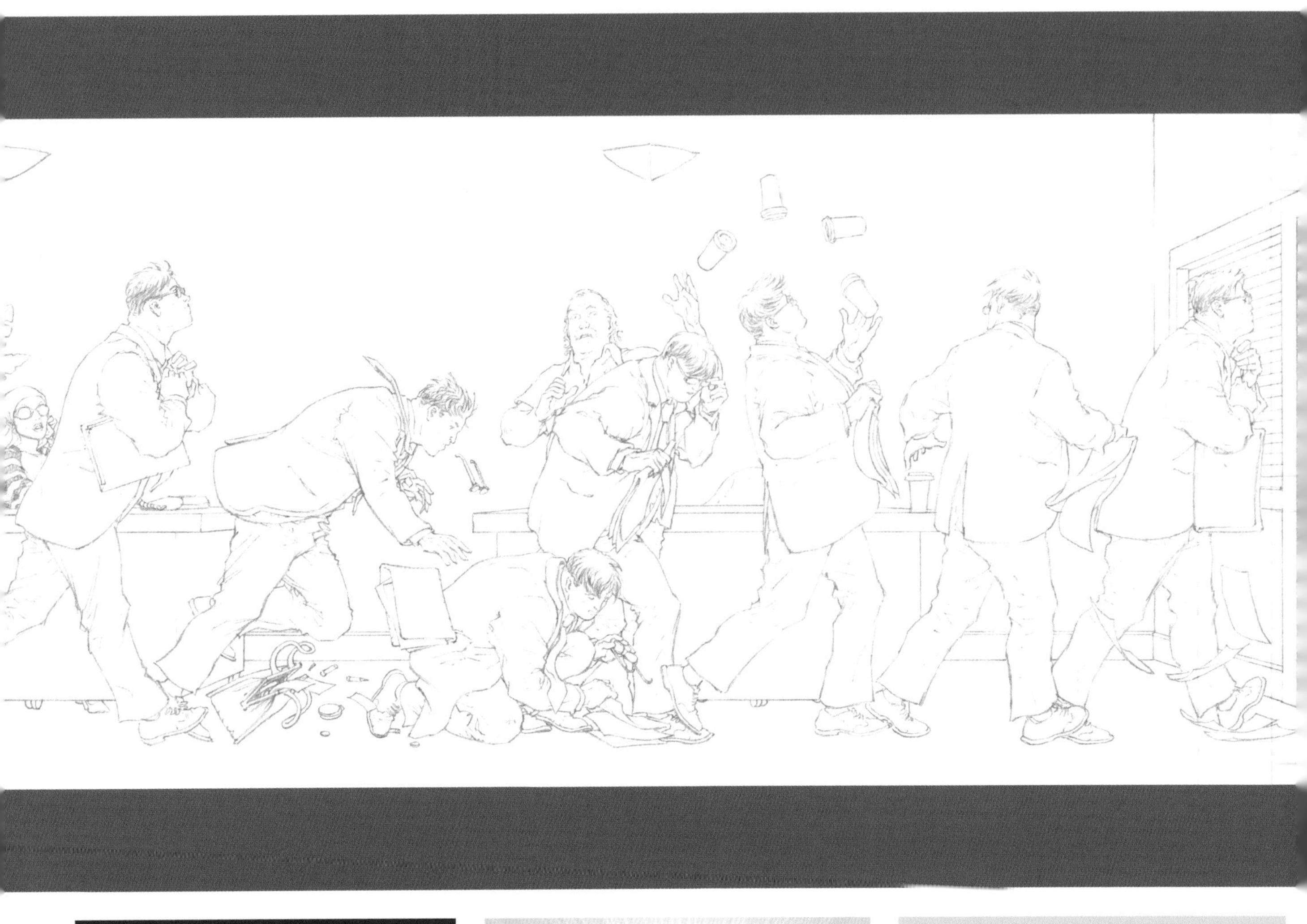

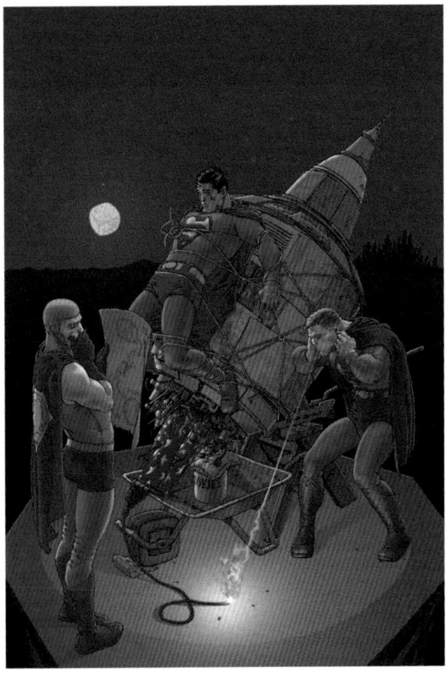

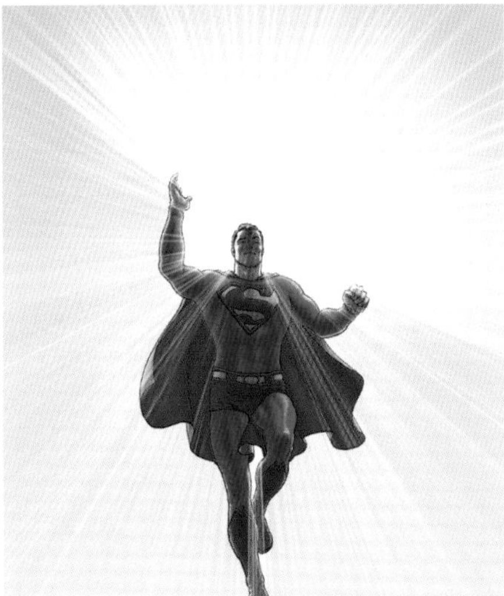

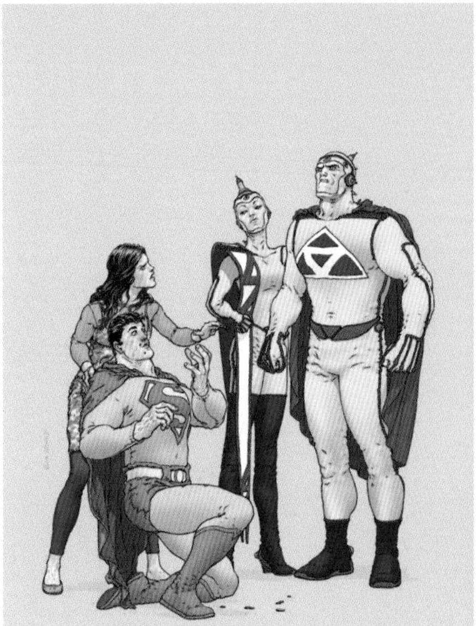

Left: *All-Star Superman* #1 (writer: Grant Morrison, DC Comics, 2005) p.9, selected panel. Pencil.

Right: *JLA: Earth 2* (writer: Grant Morrison, DC Comics, 2000) cover design. Pencil.

Below (left to right):
*All-Star Superman* #8 (writer: Grant Morrison, DC Comics, 2006) cover. Full colour digital.

*Absolute All-Star Superman* (writer: Grant Morrison, DC Comics, 2010) cover sketch. Pencil over blue crayon.

*All-Star Superman* #9 (writer: Grant Morrison, DC Comics, 2006) cover. Full colour digital.

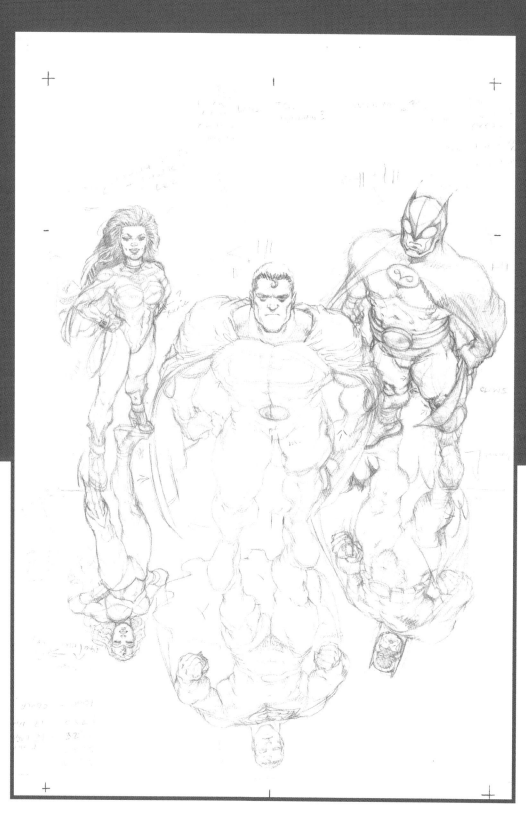

SUPERMAN

# PAX AMERICANA

Right: *The Multiversity: Pax Americana*, 'In Which We Burn' (writer: Grant Morrison, one-shot, DC Comics, 2015) pp.12-13. Finished art, full colour digital.

In this double page spread we see the threads of three different timelines – a conversation, a murder and the following investigation – playing out in a single space, made distinct with the use of different lighting in each.

Far right: *The Multiversity: Pax Americana*, 'In Which We Burn' (writer: Grant Morrison, one-shot, DC Comics, 2015) pp.1-3. Pencil over blue crayon.

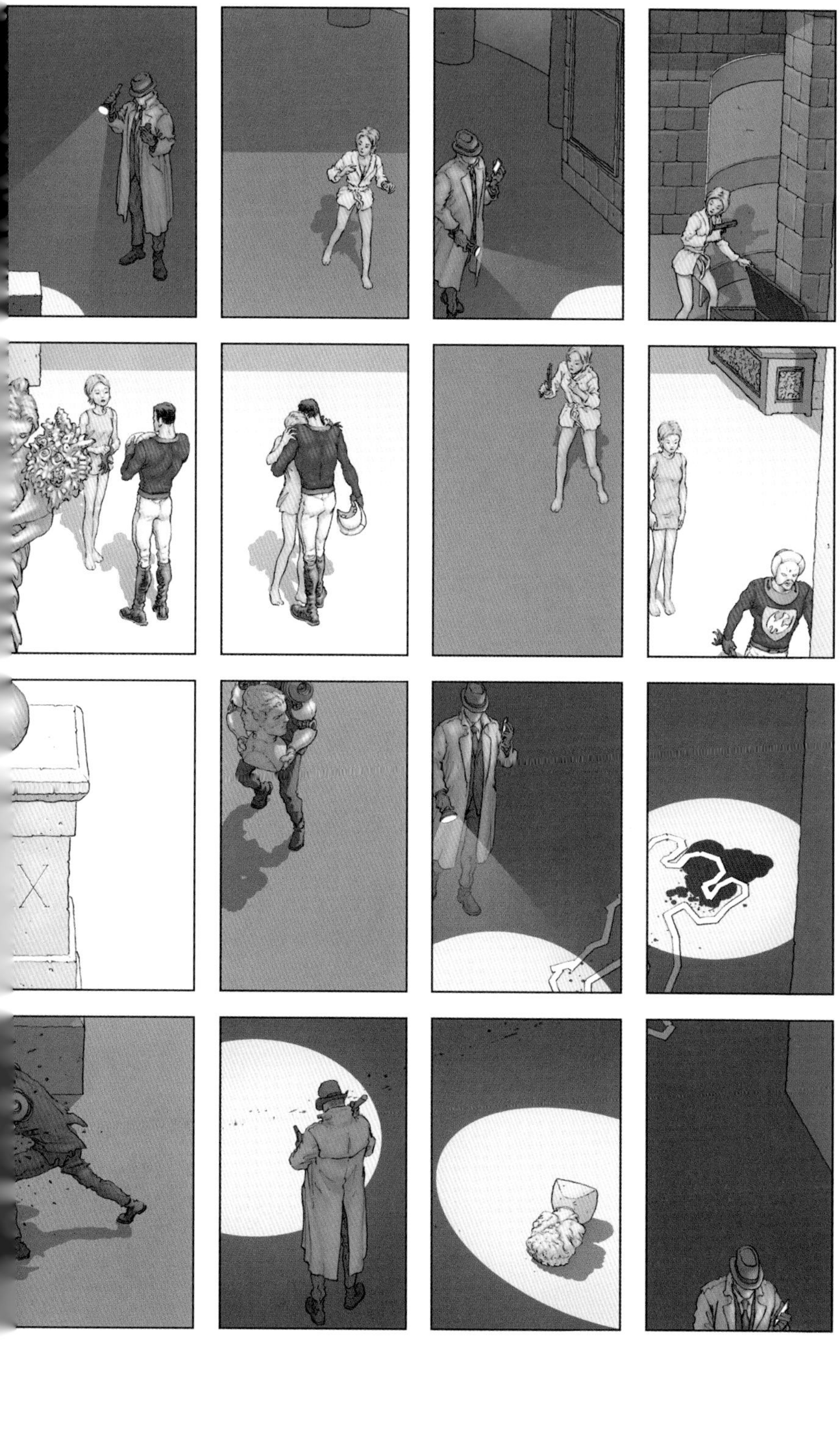

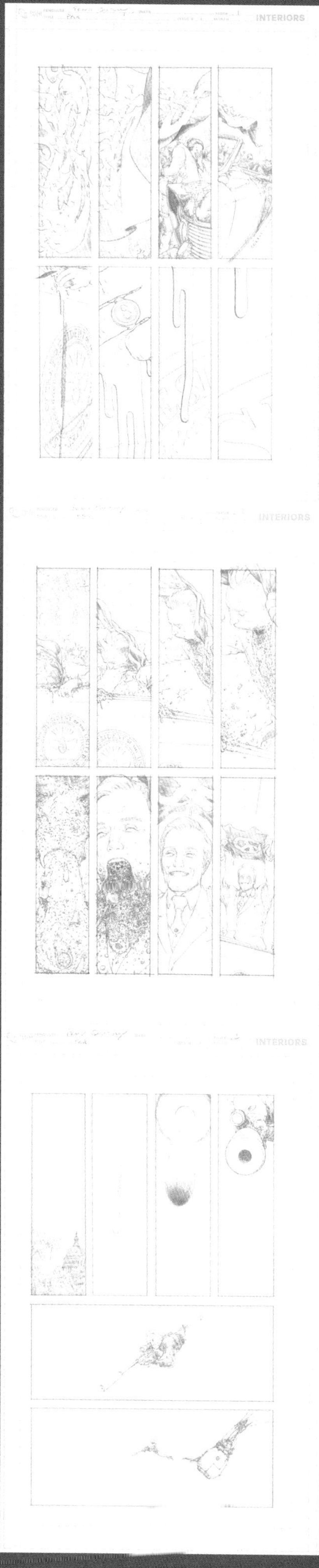
INTERIORS
INTERIORS
INTERIORS

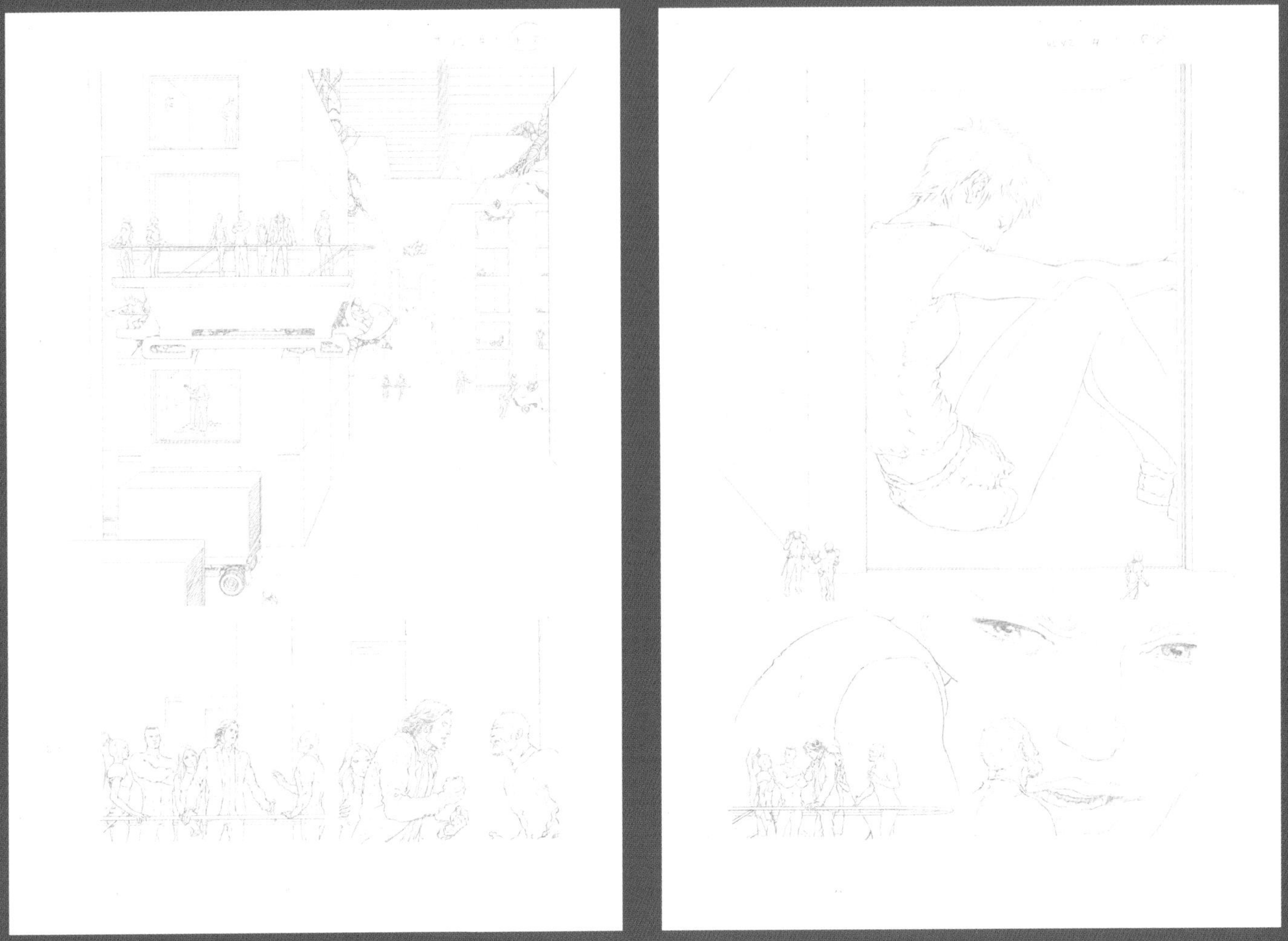

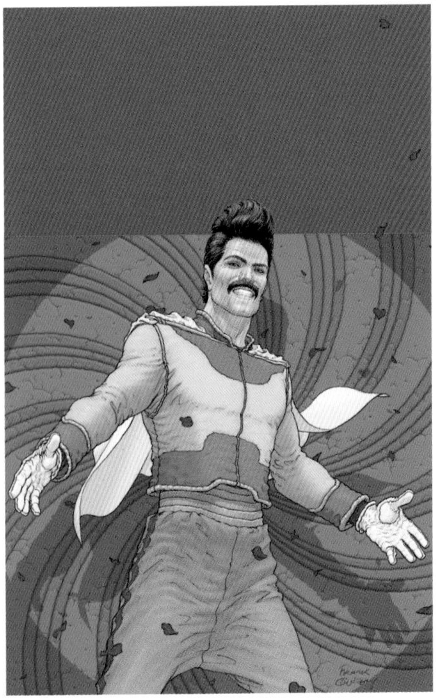

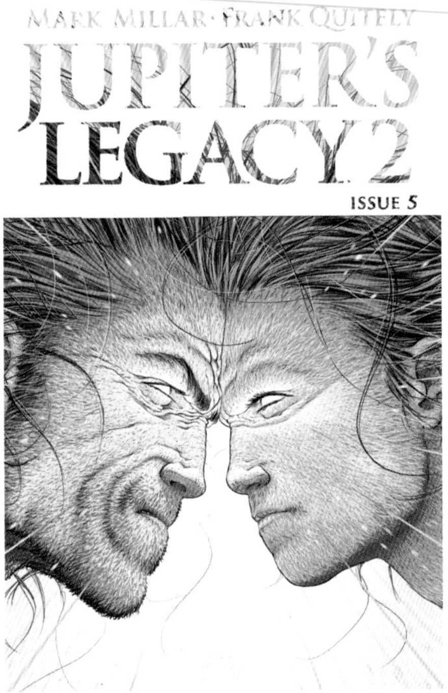
MARK MILLAR · FRANK QUITELY
JUPITER'S LEGACY 2
ISSUE 5

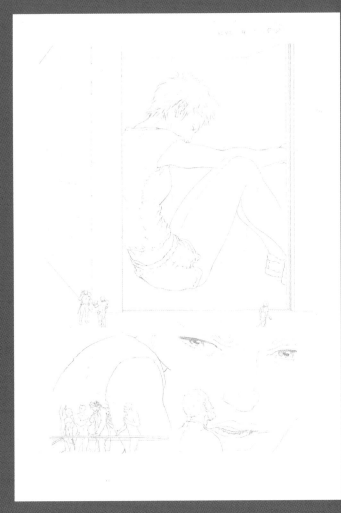

Above: ***Jupiter's Legacy*** vol.2, #1 (writer: Mark Millar, Image, 2016) pp.17-18. Pencil over blue crayon.

Far left: ***Jupiter's Legacy*** vol.2, #2, (writer: Mark Millar, Image, 2016) cover. Finished art, full colour digital.

Left: ***Jupiter's Legacy*** vol.2, #5 (writer: Mark Millar, Image, 2017) cover. Finished art, full colour digital.

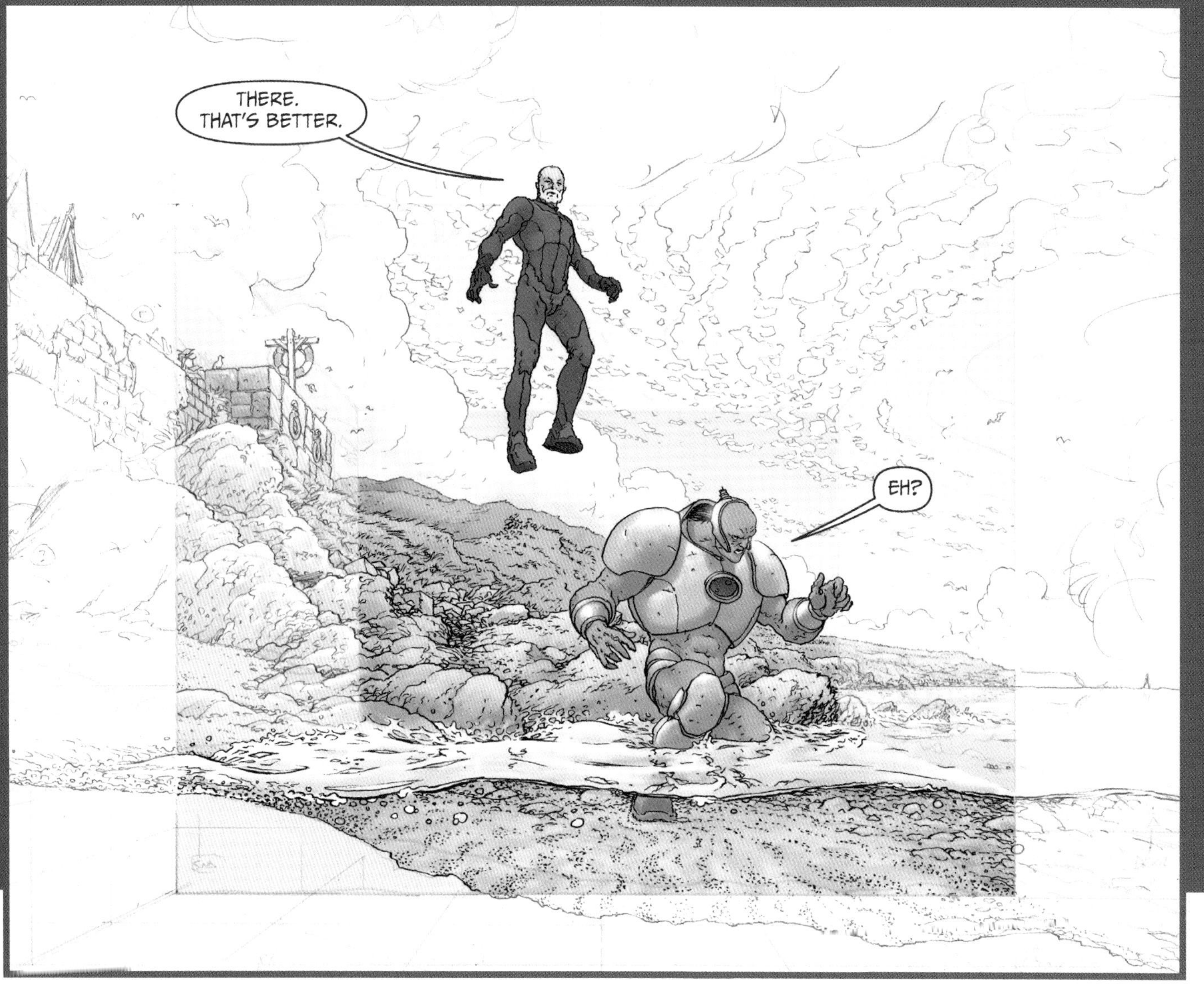
THERE. THAT'S BETTER.
EH?

Above: ***Jupiter's Legacy*** vol.1, #1 (writer: Mark Millar, Image) p.13. Finished art, full colour digital.

Here, Quitely depicts a 'psychic prison cell' by showing the comic book process of rough sketch to finished piece, suggesting that both the 'psychic prison cell' and the comic panel are constructs of memory and imagination.

# JUPITER'S LEGACY

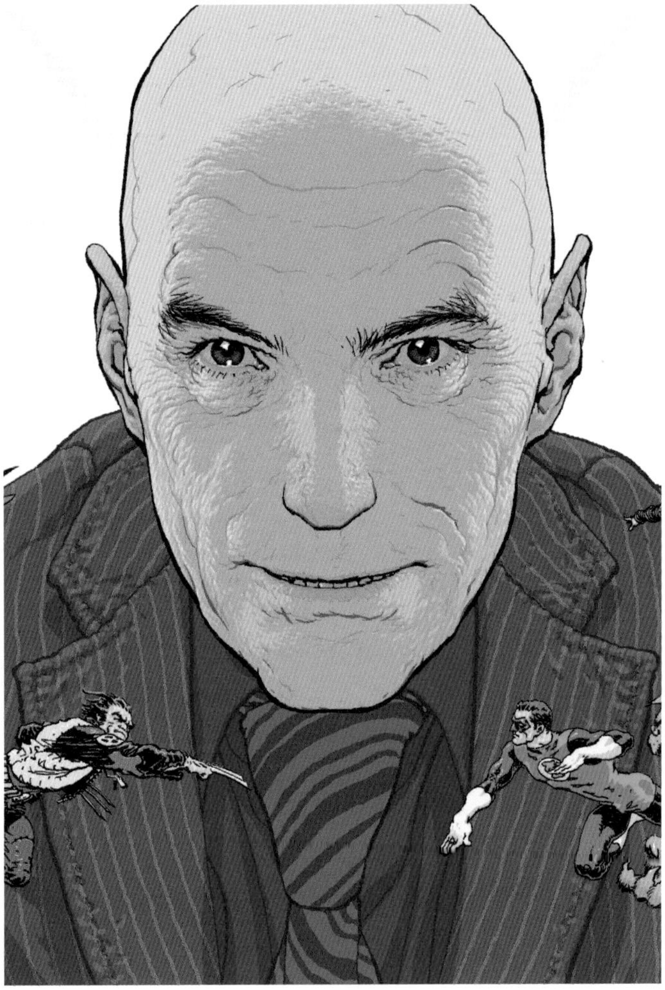

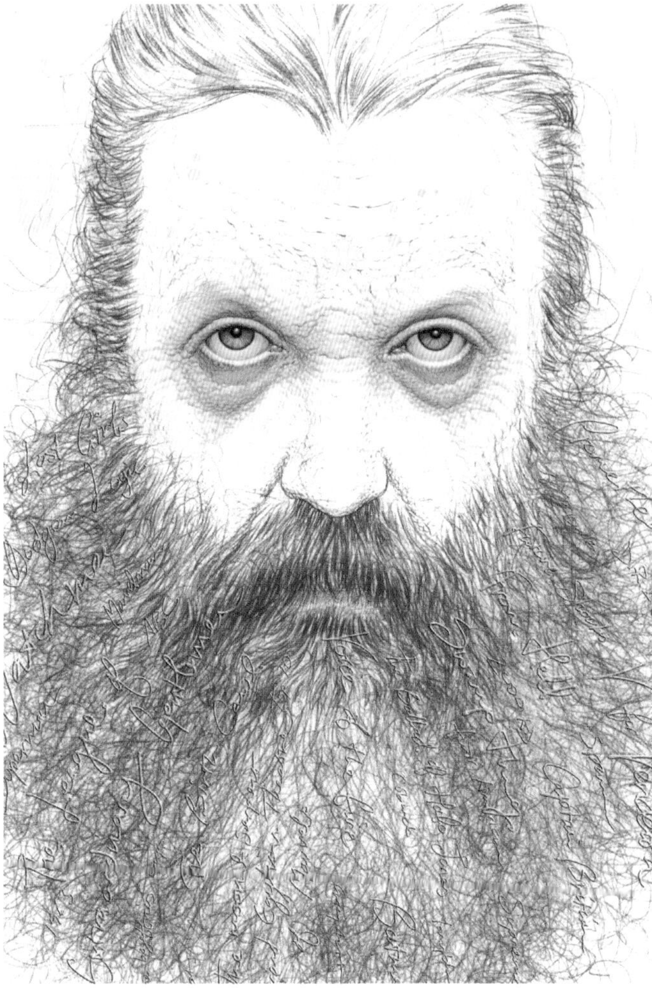

Above (from left to right):
'The Super Psyche of Comic Book Shaman Grant Morrison' in ***Playboy*** (writer: Gavin Edwards, Playboy Enterprises, May 2012) illustration for profile. Finished artwork, full colour digital.

***Alan Moore*** (2017) illustration. Finished artwork, full colour digital

***The Walking Dead***, #100 (writer: Robert Kirkman, Image, 2012) cover variant. Finished artwork, full colour digital.

***Jonah Hex***, #1 (writer: Justin Grey, DC Comics, 2006) cover. Ink, watercolour and gouache.

MISCELLANEOUS

# THE GORBALS VAMPIRE

Above: **The Gorbals Vampire** (The Citizens Theatre, 2016) sketch for cover illustration. Pencil.

Right: **The Gorbals Vampire** (The Citizens Theatre, 2016) cover illustration. Finished artwork, full colour digital.

In 1954, Glasgow's Southern Necropolis provided the backdrop for a real life vampire hunt as hundreds of children - armed with homemade weapons - stalked an iron-toothed vampire they believed to be terrorizing their neighbourhood. The resulting uproar led to strict censorship measures being put in place to target the horror comics blamed for the incident and the resulting 'Children and Young Person's (Harmful Publication) Act' is still in place today. Here, Quitely's illustration provides a poster for a community theatre production commemorating the tale.

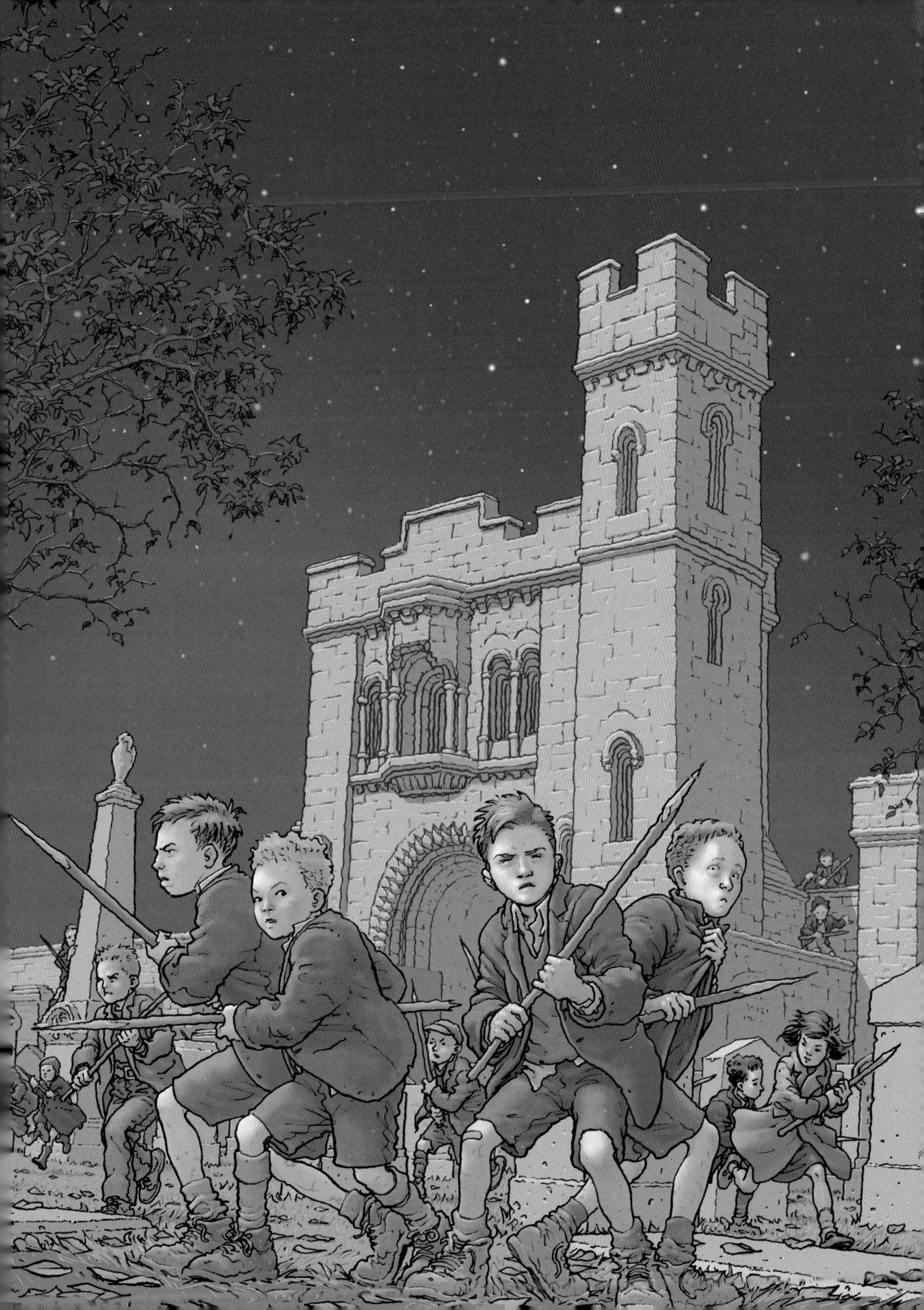

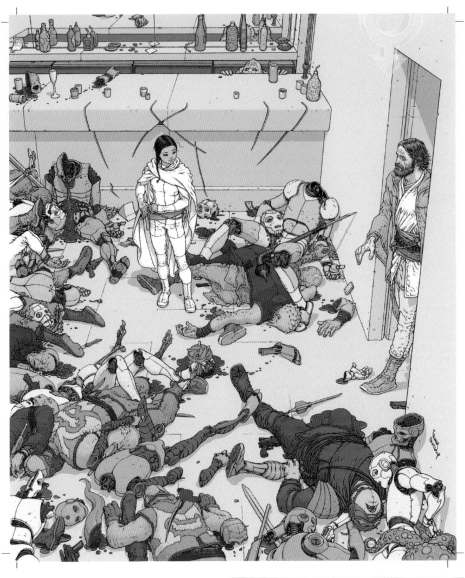

Above: 'My Padawan' in *Star Wars Art: Comics*
(Abrams Books, 2011) original illustration. Finished
artwork, full colour digital.

Opposite page: *Daredevil*, #50 (writer: Roy
Thomas, Marvel, 2011) p36. Finished artwork, full
colour digital.

Right: *Wonder Woman*, #27 (writer: Gail Simone,
DC Comics, 2009) variant cover. Finished artwork,
full colour digital.

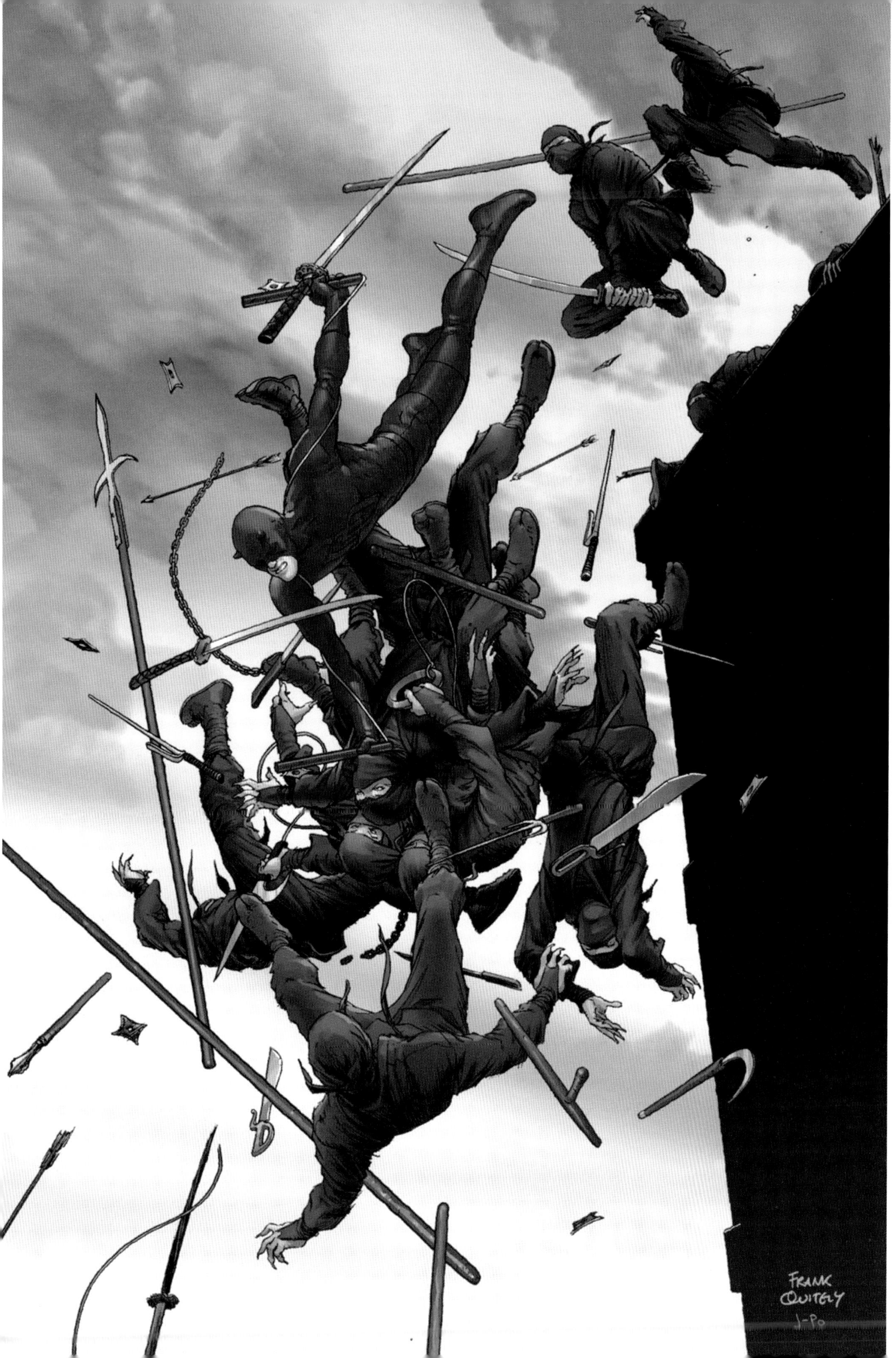
FRANK QUITELY
J-Po

***Electric Soup*** , "The Greens" #1, cover art. © John Brown Publishing.
***Judge Dredd Megazine***, vol.2. "Salvation at the Last Chance Saloon" #29, p.24, selected panel. © Rebellion Developments.
***Judge Dredd Megazine***, vol.2. "Shimura" #37, p.23. © Rebellion Developments.
***Gangland***. "Your Special Day" #1, p.2. © Vertigo (DC Comics).
***Strange Adventures***, vol.2. "Immune" #1, p.2. © Vertigo (DC Comics).
***The Big Book of Weirdos***, 'Dali', p.2. © Vertigo (DC Comics).
***The Big Book of Freaks***. "The Elephant Man", p.39. © Vertigo (DC Comics).
***The Big Book of Martyrs***. "St Polycarp: The Cult of Saints", p.48. ©Vertigo (DC Comics).
***Flex Mentalo***, #4, p.6. © Vertigo (DC Comics).
***Flex Mentalo***, #1, p.9. © Vertigo (DC Comics).
***Flex Mentalo***, #2, p.5. © Vertigo (DC Comics).
***Batman: The Scottish Connection***, pp.7, 22. © DC Comics.
***Batman and Robin*** #1, p.18. © DC Comics.
***Batman and Robin*** #1, p.22. © DC Comics.
***Batman and Robin*** vol.1. "Batman Reborn" #1-3, cover. © DC Comics.
***Batman Incorporated*** #1, variant cover. © DC Comics.
***All Star Batman with Robin the Boy Wonder***, variant cover. © DC Comics.
***New X-Men*** vol.1, #114, cover. © Marvel.
***New X-Men***, vol.1. #121, cover. © Marvel.
***New X-Men***, vol.1. #122, p.12. © Marvel.
***The Sandman: Endless Nights***. "Chapter VII: Destiny", pp.1, 3 ,6-7. © Vertigo (DC Comics).
***The Sandman: Endless Nights***. "Chapter VII: Destiny", retail poster © Vertigo (DC Comics).
***We3: The Deluxe Edition***, pp.54-55. © Vertigo (DC Comics).
***We3: The Deluxe Edition***, cover. © Vertigo (DC Comics)
***All-Star Superman***. #1, p.9, selected panel. © DC Comics.
***JLA: Earth 2***, cover design sketch. © DC Comics.
***All-Star Superman***. #8, cover. © DC Comics.
***All-Star Superman: Absolute***, cover. © DC Comics.
***All-Star Superman***. #9, cover. © DC Comics.
***The Multiversity: Pax Americana***. "In Which We Burn", pp.1-3,12-13. © DC Comics
***Jupiter's Legacy***, vol.2. #1, pp.17-18. © Image, Grant Morrison.
***Jupiter's Legacy***, vol.2. #2, cover. © Image, Grant Morrison.
***Jupiter's Legacy***, vol.2. #5, cover. © Image, Grant Morrison.
***Jupiter's Legacy***, vol.2. #1, p13. © Image, Grant Morrison.
'The Super Psyche of Comic Book Shaman Grant Morrison' in ***Playboy***, illustration for profile. © Playboy Enterprises.
***Alan Moore***, illustration. © Frank Quitely
***The Walking Dead***, #100, cover variant. © Image, Robert Kirkman.
***Jonah Hex***, #1, cover. © DC Comics.
***The Gorbals Vampire***, sketch for cover illustration. © Frank Quitely
***The Gorbals Vampire***, cover illustration. © Frank Quitely
'My Padawan' in ***Star Wars Art: Comics***, original illustration. © Abrams Books.
***Daredevil***, #50, p36. © Marvel.
***Wonder Woman***, #27, variant cover. © DC Comics.

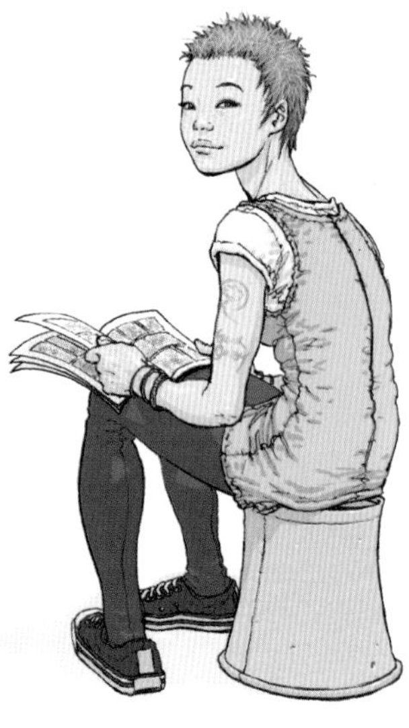

# IMAGE CREDITS